PASSAGE TO CHICAGO

A Journey on the Illinois & Michigan Canal in the year 1860

Tom Willcockson

Acknowledgements:

This publication has been made possible through the support of the Canal Corridor Association. The author would also like to extend his thanks to the following for their assistance in authenticating details and providing useful materials helpful to the completion of this project and for reading and proofing the manuscript: Arnold Bandstra, Dennis Beischke, Cynthia and Frederick Carus, Andy Connor, Cricket Trutter Hauff, Peter Kodat, Ana Koval, John Lamb, Michele Micetich, Gregory Peerbolte, Gilbert P. Taylor, Ronald S. Vasile, Sandy Vasko, Chuck Spets, Terry Willcockson.

Thank you to our Kickstarter donors for helping us finance this book: Gerald W. Adelmann, Christopher B. Burke, Inga Carus, Amar Dave, Peter L. Kodat, Sam Lucio, Michele Enrietta Micetich, Thomas & Florence Pinn, and Mike Wagner. Donations were also received in memory of Joe Kowsky and in honor of John T. Trutter.

The author would like to extend his loving appreciation to his wife Terry Willcockson whose support throughout this project contributed enormously to its final completion.

Copyright:

Published by Canal Corridor Association

Canal Corridor Association
754 First St, LaSalle, IL 61301
Visit Our Website: www.iandmcanal.org
E-mail: admin@iandmcanal.org

Illustrations & Text by Tom Willcockson
Forward by Ronald S. Vasile

Pre-press and printing Wolverton, Cedar Falls, Iowa;
Midwest Graphics Management;

ISBN 13: 978-0-692-78862-2
Library of Congress Control Number: 2016955579

Printed in the United States of America

PASSAGE TO CHICAGO
A Journey on the Illinois & Michigan Canal in the year 1860

FORWARD

The Impact and Significance of the I&M Canal

Since the birth of the new nation, American leaders had recognized the urgent need for a network of "internal improvements" to ease the problem of continental transportation. The success of the Erie Canal, completed in 1825, marked a period of intensive canal building in the U. S. Indeed, the years from 1790-1850 have been characterized as the Canal Era. This chapter in our nation's history has been largely overlooked, as most historians have focused on the railroads as the prime force behind America's economic development in the 19th century.

The I&M Canal was the final link in a national plan to connect different regions of the vast North American continent via waterways. In the years before railroads and highways, water was the most efficient way to move people and goods. The two major water routes in America were the Great Lakes and the Mississippi River, and these two water highways almost met near Chicago. Native Americans had long known that during certain seasons it was possible to canoe from the Des Plaines River to the Chicago River and Lake Michigan. They showed French explorers Louis Jolliet and Father Jacques Marquette the route in the 1670s, and the French immediately saw that it would be possible to dig a canal to connect these two waterways.

I&M Canal packet boat

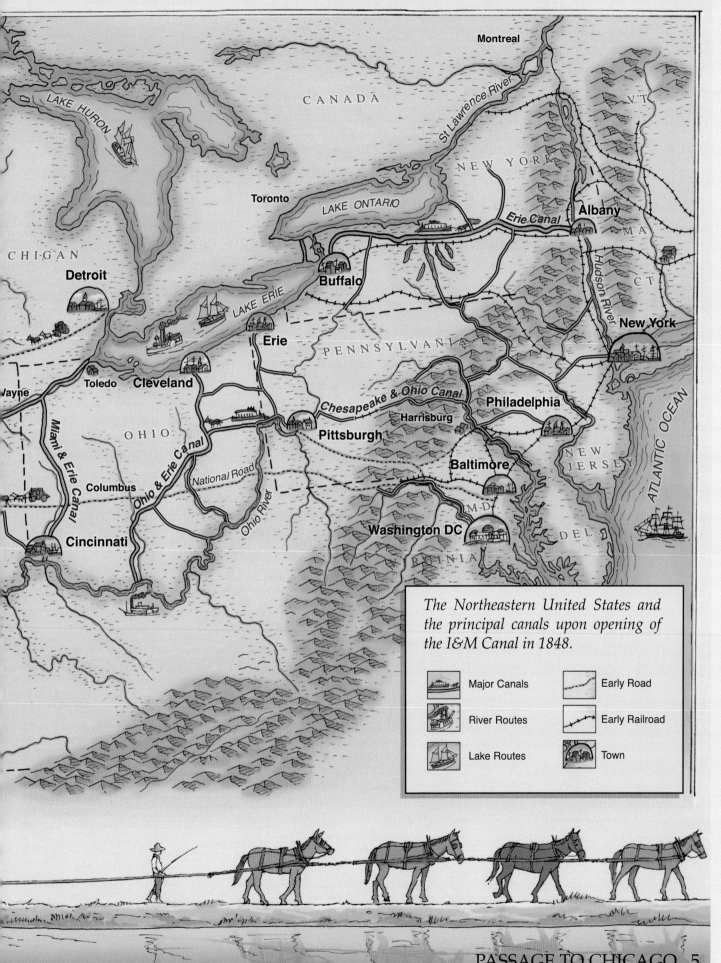

Montreal

CANADA

LAKE HURON

St Lawrence River

NEW YORK

Toronto

LAKE ONTARIO

Erie Canal

Albany

V.T.

Detroit

Hudson River

MA

CHIGAN

LAKE ERIE

Buffalo

CT

Erie

New York

PENNSYLVANIA

Wayne

Toledo

Cleveland

Chesapeake & Ohio Canal

Harrisburg

Philadelphia

ATLANTIC OCEAN

Miami & Erie Canal

Ohio & Erie Canal

OHIO

Pittsburgh

NEW JERSEY

Columbus

National Road

Baltimore

Ohio River

M.D.

Cincinnati

Washington DC

DEL

VIRGINIA

The Northeastern United States and the principal canals upon opening of the I&M Canal in 1848.

Major Canals		Early Road	
River Routes		Early Railroad	
Lake Routes		Town	

By connecting Lake Michigan to the Illinois River, the I&M extended the water highway that the Erie Canal created from New York to the Great Lakes at Buffalo. Boats could now cross the Great Lakes to Chicago, take the I&M Canal to LaSalle, and follow the Illinois to the Mississippi River south to the Gulf of Mexico. The ultimate goal, part of the larger "American System" of Henry Clay, was to link the different regions of the country, east and west as well as north and south. This connection would make the sections economically interdependent and would hopefully lessen the sectional differences, mainly over the issue of slavery, that had become increasingly apparent by 1850.

The opening of the Illinois & Michigan Canal ushered in a new era in trade and travel for the nation. By connecting the waters of the Illinois River with those of Lake Michigan (hence the name, hereafter referred to as the I&M Canal), the canal created an all-water route from New York to New Orleans, with Chicago as the crucial mid-point. The I&M Canal, opened 23 years after the Erie Canal, was the last of the great U. S. shipping canals of the nineteenth century. Following up on the Erie's success, the I&M was the final link in a chain of waterways that helped fuel the nation's economic growth. It is no exaggeration to state that the "construction and operation of the I&M Canal from 1836 to 1848 in northeast Illinois tells one of the most significant stories in the transportation history of the United States."

The I&M Canal is one of the best-kept secrets in Illinois history. Although many have heard of the canal, its seminal role in shaping northern Illinois has not been fully appreciated. The single best published source on the canal was published nearly 100 years ago when the canal was still in operation, and its primary focus is on the canal's economic impact.

Try to imagine Illinois without Chicago and the surrounding counties. If not for the very idea of the I&M Canal, Illinois as we know it would very different. In 1818, Illinois became the 21st state, but not before a key change was made to the state's borders. Plans were already being made for the proposed canal, but the original boundaries of the state would have meant that the canal would be spread over two states. In order for the new state to have a commercial outlet on Lake Michigan, the border was moved approximately forty miles to the north, adding an area about equal to the size of Connecticut. The change ensured that the canal would be under the jurisdiction of one state. Thus, Illinois statehood and the canal were advocated together. Wisconsin later attempted to regain this land, to no avail.

Much of the good work done by the canal occurred before it ever opened. In 1827 the Federal Government gave the State of Illinois 284,000 acres of land along the route of the canal to help finance its construction. When the I&M Canal Commissioners began selling this land, thousands of people began settling along the line of the canal, realizing the American dream of owning property.

The prospect of the canal brought people and eastern capital to Chicago and the surrounding region. Before the canal the site of Chicago consisted of a lonely military outpost (Fort Dearborn) situated in a swampy region. The I&M Canal Commissioners were responsible for the development of a number of towns along the proposed waterway, including Chicago, Ottawa, Lockport, Morris, and LaSalle.

The most massive public works project ever attempted in the young state of Illinois, digging began on the 4th of July in 1836. Many hoped the canal could be completed in a few years, but in 1837 the nation suffered its first major Depression, and by 1840 Illinois teetered towards bankruptcy. Work on the canal largely ceased until investors, many from Europe, came up with $1.6 million to jump-start the stalled project in 1845. It took twelve years of on again, off again labor to construct the canal, which finally opened in April of 1848.

Few today think of Illinois as part of the West, but in 1848 it was routinely referred to as such, and the I&M Canal is a symbol of America's westward expansion. The opening of the canal signaled the end of the frontier era in Chicago's history, as the city now became a gateway to the West. For example, many who sought their fortunes in the California Gold Rush of 1849 took part of their trip on an I&M canal boat. In addition to the opening of the canal, several others watershed moments occurred in Illinois in 1848, including the first telegraph line linking Chicago to the east; the first railroad in Chicago; and the establishment of the Chicago Board of Trade, prompted in part by the prospects of increased trade due to the canal. Also that year, the United States concluded a war with Mexico, acquiring large tracts of land that would lead to increased sectional tension.

The canal was 96 miles long, stretching from Bridgeport, then near Chicago, to LaSalle. It was a minimum of sixty feet wide, with several areas known as widewaters where it was twice that width. The canal had a minimum depth of six feet, although in many places it was much deeper. While we may think of northern Illinois has flat and featureless, there is a 141 foot change in elevation between Lake Michigan and the Illinois River, necessitating seventeen locks. There were also numerous bridges, aqueducts, and feeder canals to supply water. The canal operated seasonally, usually from sometime in March or April until November or December. Teams of mules pulled the 150 ton, one hundred foot long boats.

During the first five years it operated (1848 to 1852) the canal had no direct competition from railroads. A booming business in passenger travel developed, bringing people together from all walks of life. By 1853 railroads paralleled the canal route. Trains could run year round and were faster, albeit more dangerous, and they quickly took away the canal's passenger traffic. However, the canal continued to prosper and successfully competed with the railroads in the shipping of heavy bulk goods. The canal was also seen as a more democratic form of commerce, as anyone with the means could register a boat and do business on the canal, whereas the railroads were a monopoly. The canal remained the least expensive way to ship bulk cargo like grain, coal, lumber and stone.

By 1860, the canal had been operating for twelve years, and in the many towns on the line of the canal its presence was pervasive, with the canal serving as a central feature of daily life. While it fueled the growth of northern Illinois, most in Chicago were probably unaware of the canal in operation. The canal terminus at 28th and Halsted was in Bridgeport, still a suburb of Chicago. But the canal was in the news quite a bit that year, although not always for positive reasons.

At 84 years old, America was still a young country in 1860. Some people were still living who had witnessed the American Revolution. The United States had 31 million people, four million of them slaves. There were 33 states, with Oregon being the latest to join the fold in 1859. Chicago ranked ninth in population among cities at 112,172, behind fellow Western cities Cincinnati and St. Louis. Chicago would soon pass both.

The twelve years after the opening of the I&M Canal were ones of tremendous growth in northern Illinois. In 1850 Illinois was the 11th most populous state. Ten years later the population had doubled to 1.7 million and Illinois had vaulted to 4th place, behind only New York,

Pennsylvania and Ohio and having passed Virginia, Tennessee, Massachusetts, Indiana, Kentucky, Georgia and North Carolina.

The I&M Canal deserves credit for some of this growth, though while generally considered to be a success, it had not fulfilled all of the hopes of its backers. As with any new improvement there were some growing pains. Breaks in the canal slowed or even halted shipping. Mother Nature did not always cooperate and often there was too much water or not enough. Floods in 1849 and 1857 washed away bridges and the canal banks and even destroyed canal boats. The feeder canals did not always provide enough water, meaning that boats could not carry full loads. The biggest hurdle stemmed from an occasional lack of water in the Illinois River, which prevented southern trade from reaching LaSalle in the volume that had been hoped.

The flow of goods from the South reached a peak in the mid 1850s and then began to fall. Sugar was one of the most popular items from the South, and sugar tolls hit a high in 1854 before decreasing dramatically. Molasses experienced a similar trajectory, with local production a factor by 1860. To fight this loss of business, the Canal Board cut toll rates for some Southern goods in 1860 including raw cotton in bales, tobacco, molasses, sugar, and hemp.

For its first five years the canal operated without competition from the railroads. That changed in 1853 when the Chicago and Rock Island line came to LaSalle, paralleling the canal and literally a stone's throw away at LaSalle. The passenger trade on the canal, which had been extremely popular, swiftly collapsed. Some feared that the canal itself would soon suffer a similar fate but it stayed in operation until 1933.

The canal stimulated a variety of economic enterprises in northern Illinois. There was no limestone carried on the canal in its inaugural season of 1848. In 1860 over 90,000 tons of limestone were transported and coal shipments more than doubled in the first twelve years, to 11,000 tons. The national economic depression known as the Panic of 1857 did not hurt the canal immediately but revenues dropped off by $60,000 in 1859 and stayed flat in 1860.

There were relatively few glitches on the canal in 1860, but maintenance costs and repairs were higher than usual. An embankment near Lock 12 failed and detained traffic and there were the usual adjustments to aqueducts and lock gates. The canal opened earlier than it ever had before, on March 8th, and remained in business until November 26th.

The canal usually closed for the winter in late November or early December. Repairs and routine maintenance on bridges, culverts, and aqueducts were done during the winter as weather permitted and the water was drawn off some sections of the canal. Life along the canal slowed until the canal opened again in the spring. Parts of the canal still saw plenty of use in the winter, however, as people laced up their ice skates to glide over the frozen water, sometimes even having races from one town to the next.

The canal was part of a much larger, integrated transportation network. With the canal closed for about four months each year, its opening in the spring was eagerly awaited. In the winter as many as 300 boats were tied up at LaSalle, waiting for the ice to melt in the spring. By late March an immense amount of freight was awaiting shipment. Often the Illinois River was already up and running while people waited impatiently for canal navigation to open.

The canal's story did not end in 1860. The coming of the Civil War in 1861 brought about some of the canal's most prosperous years, with tolls reaching a record $300,000 per year in 1865 and 1866. Tolls began to drop in the 1870s, as more freight shifted to railroads, and by the 1890s traffic on the canal had declined dramatically. The opening of the, larger and more modern, Chicago Sanitary and Ship Canal in 1900 essentially doomed the I&M to irrelevance. The canal was derided as "a tadpole ditch" before finally closing in 1933. That same year Franklin D. Roosevelt assumed the Presidency during the depths of the Great Depression. One of his New Deal programs, the Civilian Conservation Corps, hired men to turn the tadpole ditch into a recreational trail, building campsites and structures such as the Starved Rock Lodge.

In the 1950s the State of Illinois began planning a series of expressways and during the planning stages one of them was called the I&M Canal Expressway. The first eight miles of what we now know as the Stevenson Expressway follow the path of the canal. Thus the canal was largely filled in and obliterated in the City of Chicago, with one small remnant remaining at 27th and Ashland, now Canal Origins Park.

In 1963, the canal became a National Historic Landmark and citizens began to advocate for the preservation of the remaining segments of the canal. In 1973, the State of Illinois created the I&M Canal State Trail from Channahon to LaSalle. In the early 1980s, the organization known today as the Canal Corridor Association mounted an extraordinary preservation campaign and in 1984 President Ronald Reagan signed legislation creating the I&M Canal National Heritage Corridor, the nation's first national heritage area. Since the I&M led the way, forty-eight additional heritage areas have been recognized by the Federal government. Clearly, this was an idea whose time had come, one that encompasses the connections between history, nature, recreation, tourism, and economic development.

Ronald S. Vasile
Canal Historian

Visit the I&M Canal National Heritage Area Today

Discover the legacy of those who have traveled this passageway for centuries. Stand upon the same ground traversed by Native Americans, famed explorers and French voyageurs as you walk in the footsteps of Irish canal workers and early entrepreneurs.

From grand mansions and impressive monuments to rare scenic wonders, a wealth of experiences await as you explore the fascinating stories of this living landscape.

Enjoy thousands of acres of prairies, parks and preserves containing pristine woodlands, savannas and wetlands and see what the "Prairie State" looked like to pioneer settlers when it was a virtual sea of colorful native grasslands.

Visit the historic cities and towns that owe their existence to this vital transportation corridor and discover the important connection between Abraham Lincoln and the I&M Canal. Take advantage of premier opportunities for canoeing, fishing, hiking, biking, and cross-country skiing along the I&M Canal State Trail.

Step aboard the LaSalle Canal Boat, an authentic replica, and wend your way through history on a relaxing mule-pulled ride accompanied by informative, period-dressed guides.

Start your journey to the I&M Canal National Heritage Area with a visit to the Lock 16 Visitor Center featuring a café and heritage gift shop, interpretive exhibits, and more.

Plan your visit to America's first National Heritage Area by going to iandmcanal.org or calling 815-220-1848.

Ana B. Koval, AICP, President & CEO
Canal Corridor Association

THE I&M CANAL IN 1860

By 1860, the Illinois & Michigan Canal has been in operation for 12 years and has brought settlement and prosperity to the entire region. Chicago owes its amazing growth to the canal as do many other towns along its path. The I&M Canal is the link that makes possible an all water route for commerce and trade from the eastern seaboard to the Gulf of Mexico.

The I&M Canal is 96 miles long, from the Chicago River at Bridgeport to the Illinois River at LaSalle, and changes elevation 141 feet over that distance. In 1860, the canal has 19 locks including a guard lock at Joliet and a lock to enter the Lateral Canal at Ottawa.

Heading west from Bridgeport, the first 17-mile segment, called the Summit Division, is raised above the level of the Chicago River with a lock on either end and a pumping station to supply water. Lockport to Joliet has the greatest drop in elevation, requiring 5 locks in just over 3 miles. Leaving Joliet, the canal continues down the Illinois River valley through 12 more locks, crossing four rivers via aqueducts and slack-water dams. Four feeder channels supply water to fill the canal along the way.

Travel on the I&M is much easier than on the primitive wagon roads of the time. In the early years, packet boats captured much of the passenger trade from the overland stage, but it is the mule-drawn freight boats that have created the greatest economic impact. There is now a cost-effective way for farm products to reach markets in Chicago, St. Louis, and beyond. The canal, along with the steel plow and the mechanical reaper, has encouraged settlement of the vast prairie lands beyond the Illinois River valley and helped create an agricultural revolution. An era of mechanized agriculture has begun. Towns originally laid out along the line of the I&M by the Canal Commissioners have become important ports and commercial centers for the surrounding countryside. Foremost among these growing towns is Chicago.

Bird's-eye view of the I&M Canal in 1860 showing locks, aqueducts, and feeder canals along with the towns and cities. Below is a side view profile of the canal matched to the upper map.

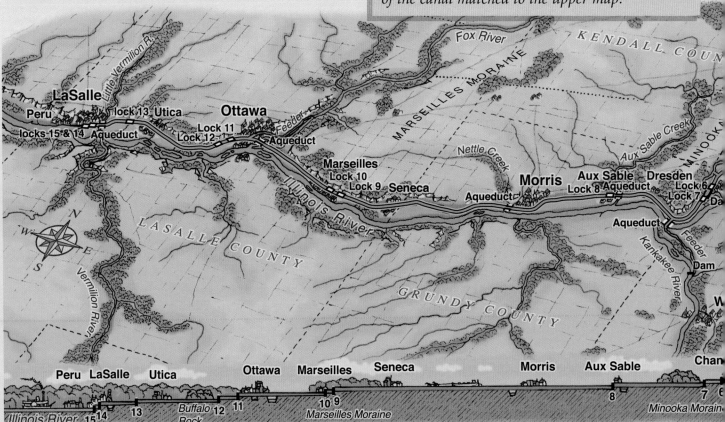

Prairie farms demand material for barns and fences. The lumberyards along the Chicago River supply enormous quantities of pine, shipped in on fleets of schooners from Michigan and Wisconsin. Freight boats take the lumber back down the canal on their return trips. Stone and coal discovered during construction of the canal supply building materials and fuel for new factories and industries.

Railroads are being built out of Chicago and competing with the canal for cargoes. The packet boats have gone out of business, and time-sensitive goods like store merchandise and pork now go by rail. However, the canal continues to prosper and compete by shipping bulk products such as corn, wheat,

lumber, coal, and stone. These are the main cargoes now being carried on the Illinois & Michigan Canal.

The pages that follow offer an illustrated account of a fictional canal boat as it travels the Illinois & Michigan Canal from LaSalle-Peru to Chicago in the Fall of 1860. This account is the author's interpretation, but great care has been taken to show the details of the journey as accurately as possible using a wide variety of resources.

CANAL BOAT AND CREW

Moored at the bank of the LaSalle Turning Basin is a canal barge named the *Prairie Star.* She is a typical lake type boat, the earliest and most common sort of cargo carrying vessel on the I&M, although the *Prairie Star* is more decorative than most in her green paint and white trim. Yesterday she delivered lumber from Chicago which is stacked up on the landing beside her; this morning she is making ready to pick up barrels of molasses and other freight from the steamboat landing, which she will take up the canal to Ottawa.

The crew of the *Prairie Star* includes the captain, Henry Dawson, who acts as steersman, and first mate Eric Lindgren, a Swedish immigrant, who works as the bowsman. This is a family-run boat, with the captain's wife Ann on board as cook, along with their two children: Maggie, a daughter who is too young to be left with relatives ashore, and their son Charlie, who helps the bowsman and his mother with chores. The boy draws no wages since he is under age 14. A mule team and driver will be hired to tow the boat out of LaSalle, completing the crew.

Freight vessels on the canal are made to carry a variety of cargoes: bulk lumber, grain, corn, or stone. They can also carry mixed cargoes of barrels, sacks, and crates. Occasionally they may even transport a

Captain Dawson of the Prairie Star supervises his son Charlie at the tiller while the first mate prepares a towline for a team of mules to move the boat down beside the steamboat landing. The captain's wife Ann is not pleased that their young daughter Maggie has come up on deck to play.

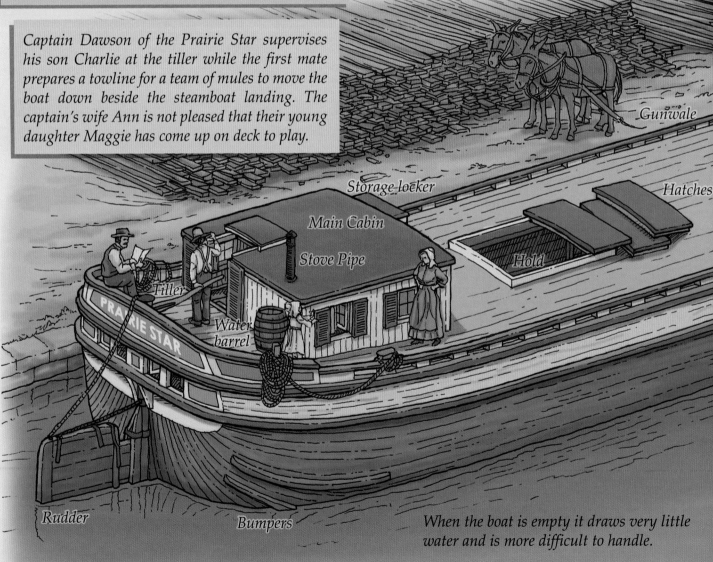

Gunwale

Storage locker

Main Cabin

Stove Pipe

Hatches

Hold

Tiller

PRAIRIE STAR

Water barrel

Rudder

Bumpers

When the boat is empty it draws very little water and is more difficult to handle.

settler's wagons and other farm equipment on deck. The design of the boat is dictated by the depth of the canal and the size of the locks. The hull is a large box-like chamber, about 100 feet long and 17 feet wide, built to maximize cargo capacity. The bow and stern are tapered for easier passage through the water; The hull is a little over 6 feet high and draws about 4 feet of water when fully loaded with over 100 tons of cargo. Bumpers along the sides of the boat and at the bow strengthen the hull and protect it in case of collision with other boats or the locks.

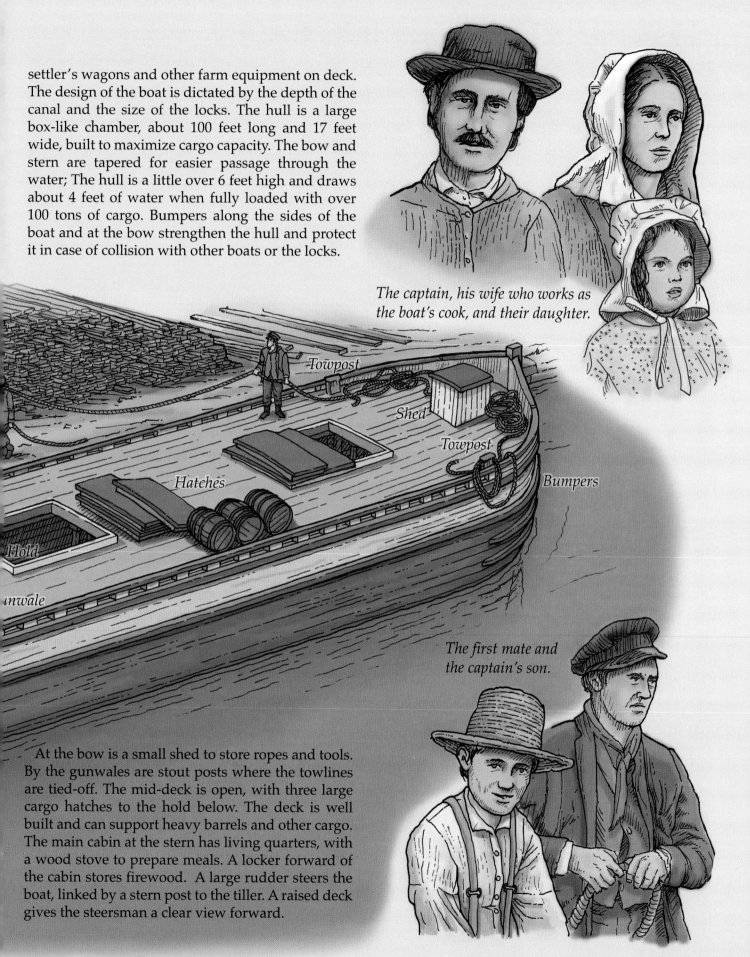

The captain, his wife who works as the boat's cook, and their daughter.

Towpost

Shed

Towpost

Hatches

Bumpers

Hold

Gunwale

The first mate and the captain's son.

At the bow is a small shed to store ropes and tools. By the gunwales are stout posts where the towlines are tied-off. The mid-deck is open, with three large cargo hatches to the hold below. The deck is well built and can support heavy barrels and other cargo. The main cabin at the stern has living quarters, with a wood stove to prepare meals. A locker forward of the cabin stores firewood. A large rudder steers the boat, linked by a stern post to the tiller. A raised deck gives the steersman a clear view forward.

THE LASALLE TURNING BASIN

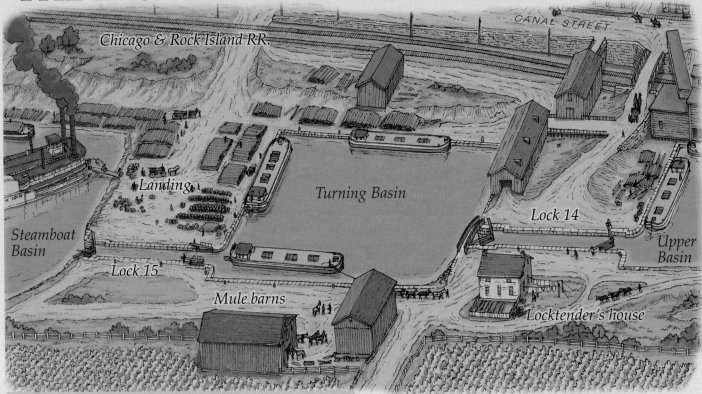

Chicago & Rock Island RR.

Canal Street

Landing

Turning Basin

Lock 14

Steamboat Basin

Upper Basin

Lock 15

Mule barns

Locktender's house

The LaSalle Turning Basin is the western terminus of the canal and its point of exchange with the Mississippi River system. Goods move across the landing to and from the Steamboat Basin or are carried by barges through Lock 15. A steamboat has come up the Illinois River from St. Louis and a gang of laborers is unloading her. Barrels and crates are hauled across a gang-plank and stacked up on the landing. The *Prairie Star* will spend most of the day loading them for delivery to Ottawa; there is much trade between towns on the canal.

Above: The Steamboat Basin, the Turning Basin and the Upper Basin, also Locks 14 & 15.

Right: Laborers move barrels from the landing to the hold of the Prairie Star. Most are Irish and German immigrants, but there are also free blacks who work as deckhands on the steamboats.

Steamboats with their wide beam and low draft are well-suited to the shallow tributaries of the Mississippi River. Boilers, engines, and paddle wheels are carried on the boiler deck, resting just above the waterline. Most of the cargo is also on this deck along with accommodations for deckhands and the poorer passengers. Well-to-do passengers travel in cabins on the hurricane deck. Above the hurricane deck is the pilot house, where the captain steers the boat and has a clear view of any snags or hazards in the river.

The value of transporting passengers and cargo by water can not be underestimated. Goods arrive at the St Louis levee from New Orleans and are loaded on steamers bound for towns along the Illinois River. At LaSalle-Peru cargo is transferred to the I&M. Returning steamboats often tow canal barges loaded with lumber and other goods. Before the railroad, passengers arriving at LaSalle might transfer to one of the horse-drawn packet boats that traveled the canal. In 1848, Abraham Lincoln, his wife Mary and sons Robert and Eddie took a packet from Chicago when returning from Washington D.C. They crossed the landing here and boarded a steamboat to Peoria.

The *Prairie Star* is moved down the bank of the Turning Basin opposite the cargo that is piled up on the landing. There is plenty of maneuvering room for canal barges in the basin. Gang-planks are set on the gunwales and men begin rolling barrels to the deck.

The cargo must be carefully loaded to fill the boat and evenly distribute the weight. Heavy molasses barrels are lowered into the hold first. Sacks of grain, bales of wool, stoneware jugs containing butter, and some full of whiskey are stowed away in the spaces above the molasses barrels. Crates of fragile merchandise are put into the hold last. Lighter barrels of flour or apples can be stowed on deck along with a couple of millstones, destined for a flour mill in Ottawa. Barrels are the universal shipping containers of the day and village coopers are kept busy making them. They can contain all kinds of products, from horse hair for stuffing furniture to delicate china packed in straw.

Barrels are stacked in the hold, with sacks of grain, bales of wool, and stoneware crocks on top.

THE MULE TEAM

As the cargo is being loaded, Captain Dawson walks over to a large barn by the Steamboat Basin to hire a team of mules to tow the *Prairie Star*. Mules are powerful, sure-footed animals and harnessed in a team they can pull a 150-ton boat. They are intelligent and even-tempered and less prone to be startled along the towpath than horses. A team of four to five mules is needed to tow heavy barges upstream, with three mules required when going down the canal. They can pull a boat at a steady two to three miles per hour but will not overwork themselves; when tired, the team simply refuses to pull any further. If treated well, a mule can work for 15 to 20 years.

A local man may drive a team for wages or hire out his own mules, with his sons as drivers.

The harnesses must be properly fitted to maximize the power of the team and to prevent chafing and painful sores or galls.

Saddle mule

Jack saddle

Trace

Trace

Wippletree

Boys as young as 14 to 17 may be hired out as mule drivers on the I&M. Often uneducated, profane and prone to theft, gambling, and fighting, they lead a rough life along the canal.

Feed baskets

Drivers lead animals into the yard and harness them in teams. Mules are hitched in tandem, one behind another, making room on the towpath for other teams to pass. They pull from the chest, with a large collar spreading the force over their shoulders. Trace straps transmit the power back to the wippletree, a wooden beam where the towline is attached.

Mules pull for four to six hours before a fresh team is needed. Barns located every 10 to 15 miles allow tired animals to be fed, groomed, and rested before towing another boat. A large barn may house a hundred mules, in stalls on the lower level with hay and grain kept above. In winter, mules may go to a local farm where sadly they are sometimes poorly fed, leaving them in weak condition by the next canal season.

Jack, a driver not much older than 15, brings the team over to the Turning Basin while the *Prairie Star* finishes loading cargo. Mule driving can be a rough business, and more than a few drivers have drowned in the canal. The most famous mule driver on the I&M was James Butler (Wild Bill) Hickok. Hickok took a job on the canal as a mule driver at age 17. In the first recorded fight of his long career, Bill tangled with a fellow canal driver, Charles Hudson, who had been abusing his mules. Bill would flee and head west were he gained fame as a lawman and gunslinger.

Mule barn

While at the barn, mules are fed hay and oats along with some corn. On the towpath they can be fed from baskets fitted over their heads.

Collar

Hip strap

Trace

Hame

Collar

Reins

Girth

Bridle

Lead mule

Lead mules are chosen for a calm and docile temperament. Bridles control the animal's head and direction of travel.

LOCK 14

Approaching Lock 14.

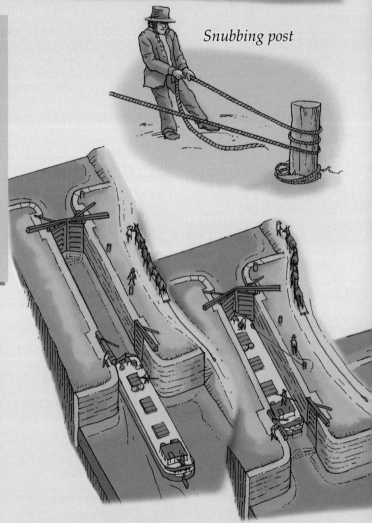

Snubbing post

After spending most of the day loading cargo, the *Prairie Star* is finally ready to exit the Turning Basin by Lock 14. Locks are massive stone chambers with wooden gates on either side which allow canal boats to enter and exit. Once a boat is within and the gates are closed, the chamber can be filled with water to raise a boat up or emptied out to lower it. The *Prairie Star* will be raised to the Upper Basin where she can start towing on the canal.

The driver whistles to the mules, coaxing them to pull the heavy boat, and slowly the *Prairie Star* begins to move. Captain Dawson blows his boat horn and calls "lock-ee!" to alert the locktender to open the gates. When the boat has enough momentum to carry it into the chamber he shouts "headway!" and the towline is cast off. The mules continue on to wait by the Upper Basin. With only inches of leeway to spare, the boat must be steered carefully. A collision can cause serious damage, although the bumpers on the hull will absorb much of the shock.

The locktenders have begun pushing the heavy balance beams to swing open the lower gates. The boat glides into the lock chamber and the bowsman tosses a line up to one of them who wraps it around a wooden snubbing post. He plays out the line to slowly bring the boat to a halt. It must be done carefully so the vessel keeps enough headway to fully enter the lock without crashing into the upper gates.

The lower gates are then closed and sluice valves for the upper gates are opened to allow water to flood the lock chamber. In 15 minutes, over 150 tons of vessel and cargo is raised 14 feet to the level of the Upper Basin. The upper gates are then opened, the towline is re-tied to one of the boat's tow posts, and the mules pull her out of the lock.

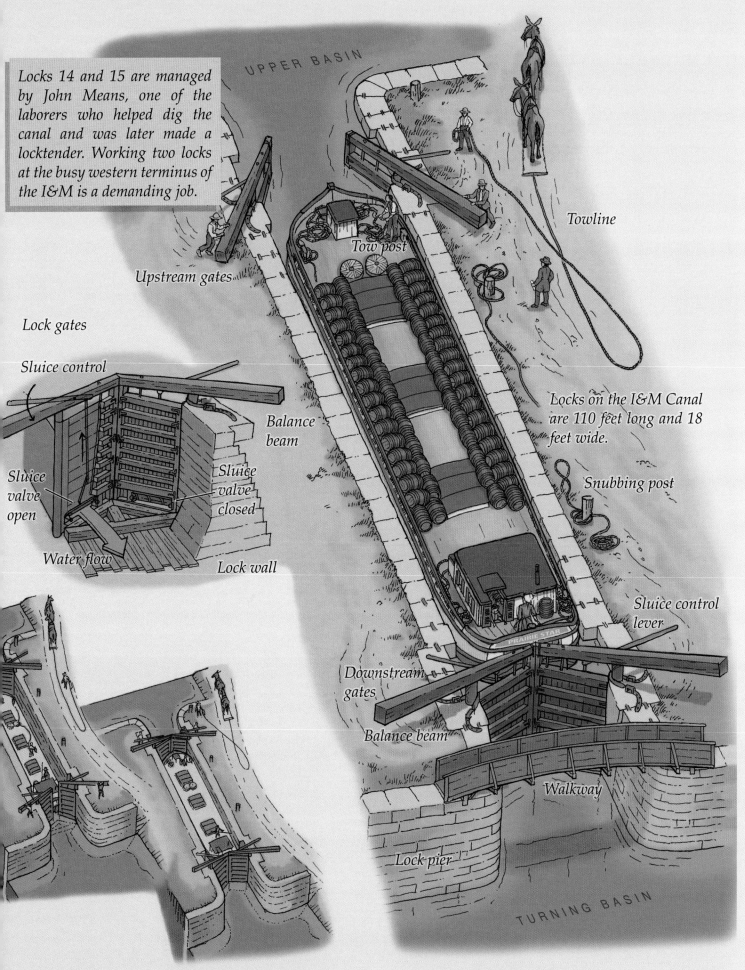

Locks 14 and 15 are managed by John Means, one of the laborers who helped dig the canal and was later made a locktender. Working two locks at the busy western terminus of the I&M is a demanding job.

UPPER BASIN

Towline

Tow post

Upstream gates

Lock gates

Sluice control

Balance beam

Sluice valve open

Sluice valve closed

Water flow

Lock wall

Locks on the I&M Canal are 110 feet long and 18 feet wide.

Snubbing post

Sluice control lever

Downstream gates

Balance beam

Walkway

Lock pier

TURNING BASIN

COAL MINING OUTSIDE LASALLE

The mules pull the boat away from Lock 14 and along the Upper Basin, approaching the LaSalle Shaft, one of the first coal mines on the canal. The growth of industry in the last decade has meant a dramatic increase in the demand for coal, particularly in Chicago. Bituminous coal was surveyed here in 1854 and the first shaft dug in 1856. Now there are several mines attracting new groups of immigrant miners to join the Irish canal workers already in LaSalle.

In a coal mine, a main shaft is dug down to the coal seam with tunnels and chambers made beyond a central supporting core. At LaSalle the coal seam is about 400 feet down. Waste rock from the excavation is piled up, contained within wooden cribbing, to support the crushing weight of the ceiling. Excess waste is taken to the surface and dumped as slag.

To get at the coal, a miner undercuts the rock below the seam and then excavates the shale above until a whole section collapses to the floor. The coal is then gathered and loaded into a mine car which is pulled by mule back to the main shaft. There the miner pushes it onto a lift and travels with it to the pit head

Lock 14

Towpath

Rock Island Railroad

Coal bunker

UPPER BASIN

Coal chute

Slag chute

Coal barge

Coal

Chicago

Fox R.

Lake Michigan

Lockport

Morris

Joliet

Ottawa

La Salle

Illinois R.

Kankakee R.

Factories

Coal mines

Canal

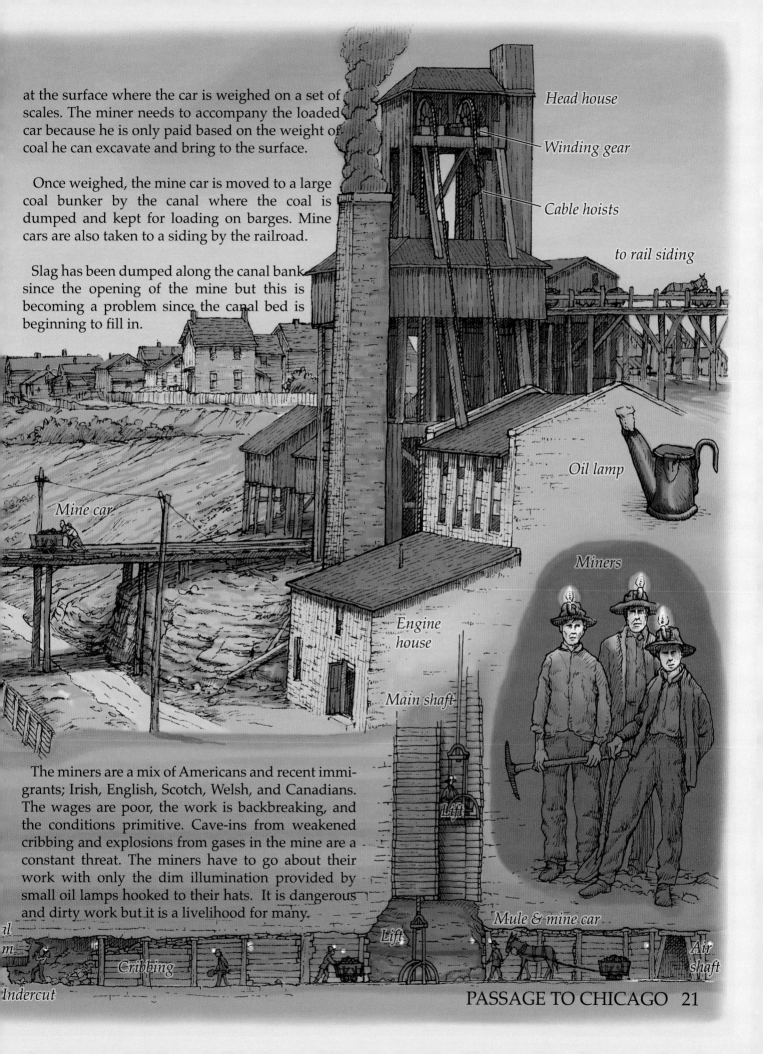

at the surface where the car is weighed on a set of scales. The miner needs to accompany the loaded car because he is only paid based on the weight of coal he can excavate and bring to the surface.

Once weighed, the mine car is moved to a large coal bunker by the canal where the coal is dumped and kept for loading on barges. Mine cars are also taken to a siding by the railroad.

Slag has been dumped along the canal bank since the opening of the mine but this is becoming a problem since the canal bed is beginning to fill in.

The miners are a mix of Americans and recent immigrants; Irish, English, Scotch, Welsh, and Canadians. The wages are poor, the work is backbreaking, and the conditions primitive. Cave-ins from weakened cribbing and explosions from gases in the mine are a constant threat. The miners have to go about their work with only the dim illumination provided by small oil lamps hooked to their hats. It is dangerous and dirty work but it is a livelihood for many.

Head house

Winding gear

Cable hoists

to rail siding

Oil lamp

Miners

Engine house

Main shaft

Lift

Mule & mine car

Lift

Cribbing

Indercut

Air shaft

THE WESTERN DIVISION

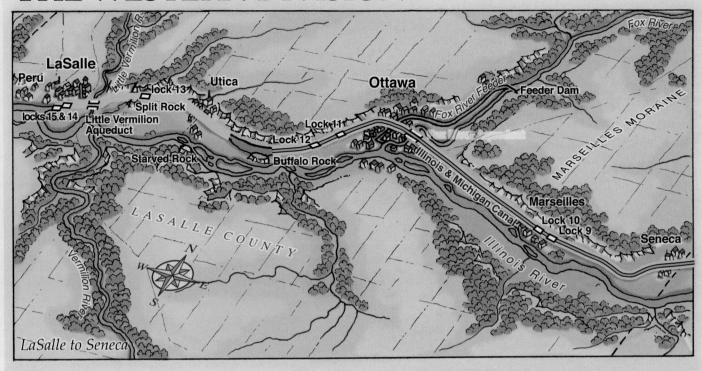

LaSalle

Perú

Little Vermilion R.

Lock 13

Utica

locks 15 & 14

Split Rock

Little Vermilion
Aqueduct

Starved Rock

Buffalo Rock

Lock 12

Lock 11

Ottawa

Fox River Feeder

Feeder Dam

Fox River

L A S A L L E   C O U N T Y

N
W   E
S

Vermilion River

Illinois & Michigan Canal

Illinois River

MARSEILLES MORAINE

Marseilles

Lock 10

Lock 9

Seneca

LaSalle to Seneca

It is late in the afternoon by the time the *Prairie Star* finally leaves LaSalle behind, setting out on the Western Division of the canal for Ottawa. There are three divisions of the I&M Canal, each with a superintendent who is responsible for its lock tenders, toll collectors, inspectors, and laborers. The principal towns of the Western Division are LaSalle, at the western terminus, and Ottawa, on the Fox River. Utica is smaller, but growing in importance. In the next 20 miles, the land will rise 51 feet requiring 5 locks. The boat will also cross two rivers via aqueducts, the first of which is just outside LaSalle across the Little Vermilion River.

Outside LaSalle, the canal crosses over the Little Vermilion River at an aqueduct. Four massive stone piers support a wooden trough that contains the water of the canal.

Aqueduct cross section

Road and rail bridge

Little Vermilion Aqueduct

Little Vermilion R.

William Gooding was the chief engineer and designer of the Illinois & Michigan Canal. He had no formal training, but learned his trade while working on the Welland and Wabash & Erie Canals. Gooding employed many of the features he learned from these earlier waterways when planning out the I&M.

A canal is a man-made channel, allowing navigation. Locks change the elevation, and the channel between two locks is called a "level." The first level on the I&M is from Lock 14 in LaSalle to Lock 13 just past Split Rock. The Little Vermilion aqueduct carries the canal over the river bed, while beyond it, earth embankments on the towpath side maintain the level above the bottomlands. The width of the canal prism averages about 60 feet, with a depth of only 6 feet.

Feeder canals are used to supply water. Without adequate replenishment, evaporation and leaks in the banks would soon cause barges to ground or be forced to carry less cargo. However, floods can cause serious damage to earthen embankments, and there are stone waste weirs on each level with overflow channels to drain away excess water.

At Split Rock, a large rocky spur in the bluff has been blasted away with black powder to make room for the level to pass right through rather than diverting the canal around this natural obstacle.

Canal prism cross section

Split Rock *Lock 13* *Utica*

Bottom land

The Chicago & Rock Island Railroad reached LaSalle in 1853. In many places trains run right beside the canal.

Chicago & Rock Island Railroad

I & M CANAL

Tow path

Bank watcher

Earthen embankments are subject to collapse, particularly if animals like muskrats burrow into them, and a washout might close the canal for months. A number of bank watchers are employed to walk the canal and trap animals in addition to making simple repairs.

Muskrats

ALONG THE TOWPATH AT SPLIT ROCK

Split Rock

Culvert

Towline

Waste Weir

By the time the boat passes through Split Rock, it is nearing sunset. Ottawa is only 10 miles away, but the late start from LaSalle means the *Prairie Star* will stop for the night before reaching there. The crew works to get her as far along as possible before dark. The mule boy is out in front with the team, while the captain steers the boat, and the bowsman makes ready for Lock 13 just ahead.

The mules pull a 300 foot towline as they tread along the towpath, passing over a culvert that carries the Pecumsaugan Creek under the canal and crossing a wood plank bridge over a waste weir. Jack the mule boy keeps them at a pace that moves the boat along at 2 to 3 miles an hour. He watches for snakes and other surprises along the towpath; one panicked animal can end with an entire team drowning in the canal. If he is seen drowsing or jay-larking, or lets the towline sag in the water, he'll earn a sharp rebuke shouted from the boat. At Lock 13, Jack will give the mules some oats from baskets fitted over their heads.

The mule boy keeps the team at a steady pace on the towpath. If he spots a snapping turtle he might try to catch him for the cook.

The steersman swings the tiller which is directly connected to the rudder. Deck cleats give leverage.

Stern Post

Tiller

Boat Horn

Deck Cleats

A mule boy remains with the team when changing at mule barns. He often sleeps in the hayloft, or in a large dormitory in town. On the towpath, he occasionally catches turtles for the stew pot; chickens or piglets can also vanish from a barnyard beside the canal if the farmer isn't watchful. Jack takes advantage of any opportunity that presents itself.

Captain Dawson is at the tiller, and keeps the *Prairie Star* to the center of the channel, making it a little easier for the mules to pull. He carefully steers past other boats and into the locks. The first mate or his wife can help out when needed. Many captains are former crewmen, some even former mule drivers. Henry Dawson looks after his boat very carefully, since he is the owner and his savings are tied up in it.

Eric the first mate works as the bowsman, assisted by Charlie the captain's son. He watches over the towline, and for any obstacles or dangers ahead, including shallow areas where the boat might ground. He looks after the cargo, coils rope, and makes repairs. If the boat is old and leaky, he may have to frequently pump the bilge. He is available to lend a hand whenever needed, particularly at locks.

The bowsman coils ropes, makes repairs, pumps the bilge, and gets the boat ready for the next lock.

The storage locker holds tools, paint, extra rope, oakum for sealing leaks, and a lantern for running at night.

Boat-Pole

Tow Post

Tow Line

THE STERN CABIN

The stern cabin is the living quarters for the family and a place to prepare meals. It is small and cramped, with little privacy, and is designed to take a minimum amount of space on the boat, space which is reserved for the all-important cargo.

Just beneath the steering deck is the stateroom, used as the family's sleeping quarters. An old curtain can be drawn across to divide the space; there isn't much privacy. Eric, the first mate, often sleeps on deck, or on the floor of the cabin in bad weather.

Small windows at the rear of the stateroom provide some fresh air, but often this space is uncomfortably hot and musty. Personal items and extra clothing are stored in sacks under the beds. On the floor is a small chamber pot. Waste is thrown right into the canal along with other trash and kitchen scraps. There is a small curtained opening as an exit.

The cabin is set low into the hull giving the steersman a clear view over the roof, and allowing unobstructed passage under bridges. The captain's wife Ann spends much of her day here getting meals ready for the crew and mending

Steering deck

Tiller

Boat horn

Tow

Fresh water barrel

Cleat

Lantern

Stateroom

Curtain

Bed

Bed

Chamber pots

Ladder

Futtock

clothing. It is hard to keep this space very clean. She also tends to the schooling of the children when time allows. Small windows don't admit much breeze, and the cabin can be stifling on hot summer days.

There is a small wood-burning stove which she tends for most of the day with a pot of coffee usually on top. A box in the corner supplies the firewood with more in a storage locker on deck. Corn cobs are used for kindling to start the fire in the morning. She uses a simple frying pan and an iron pot to do most of the cooking. A salted ham hangs from the ceiling, which she covers in cloth to keep off the flies.

Along the walls is storage space for food and other items needed for meals: casks of apples and lard, sacks of corn meal and flour. There are also vegetables, potatoes, and sometimes a loaf of bread purchased from a locktender. Shelves hold tinware plates and utensils, bottles, and candles. Tobacco and coffee beans are carefully stored on a shelf with a coffee grinder.

Charlie brings a bucket of water to his mother from the fresh water barrel on the steering deck. Maggie has awoken from a nap in the stateroom and wants to come up. She keeps well away from the hot wood stove, having learned not to touch it.

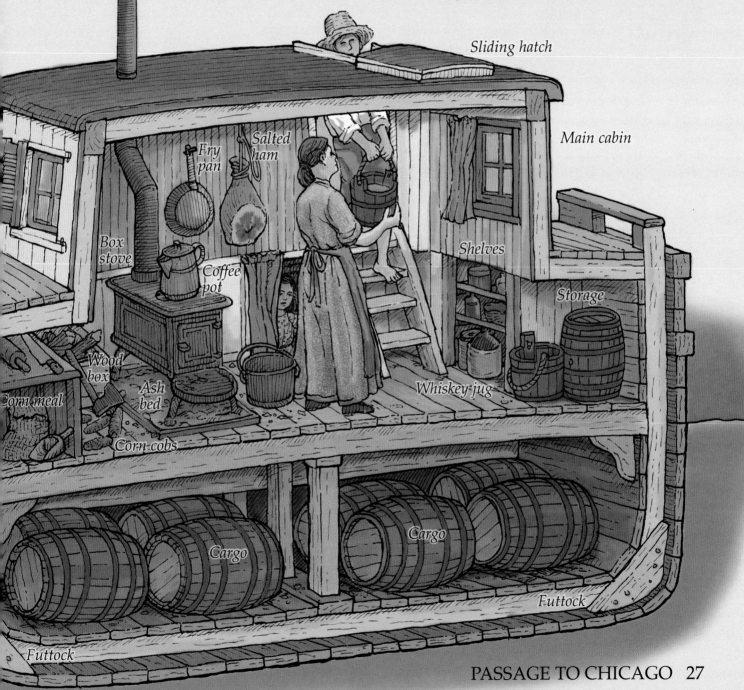

Sliding hatch

Main cabin

Fry pan

Salted ham

Box stove

Coffee pot

Shelves

Storage

Wood box

Ash bed

Corn meal

Corn cobs

Whiskey jug

Cargo

Cargo

Futtock

Futtock

NORTH UTICA, HYDRAULIC CEMENT

Workers break up lime rock above the caustic smoke of burning kilns. After heating, the gravel is shoveled out below, taken to the mill and ground into powder.

Lime kilns

Cement mill

Engine house

Wood fuel stacked up to supply the kilns.

Loading cement barrels

Two miles past Lock 13, the *Prairie Star* arrives at the village of North Utica. The sun is just setting and the oil lamps are being lit, as smoke rises from James Clark's cement plant on the northern outskirts of town. North Utica is small and the boat reaches the center of town within minutes, gliding beneath a sturdy iron truss bridge used by horse drawn mine cars to cross the canal. Next to the bridge is a stone warehouse, also belonging to Clark, where a barge is loading barrels of cement and sack grain in the fading light.

During the construction of the I&M, a high quality hydraulic lime was discovered nearby, and a mill was established to make hydraulic cement for the canal. Hydraulic cement is a masonry mortar which is very durable in water and essential to locks and dams and other canal structures. In 1845 James Clark purchased the mill to sell the cement to the public which was an immediate commercial success for him. He soon relocated and expanded the plant on the north side of town.

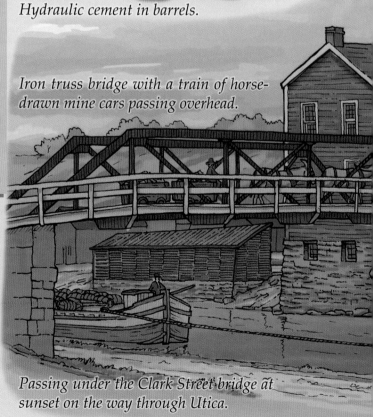

Hydraulic cement in barrels.

Iron truss bridge with a train of horse-drawn mine cars passing overhead.

Passing under the Clark Street bridge at sunset on the way through Utica.

James Clark was born in England in 1811 and came to America as a young man, eventually settling near Utica. In 1842 he became a contractor for the canal, where he realized the commercial potential of the hydraulic cement mill. He built the stone warehouse in 1849 to take advantage of the canal traffic and to ship out his cement. North Utica is a kind of company town; its main avenue is named Clark Street.

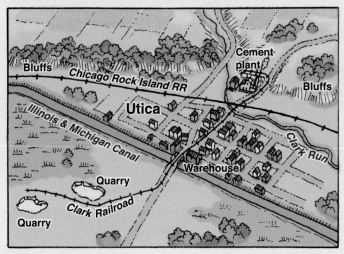

Map of North Utica

Clark's stone warehouse and general store. Cement barrels are being loaded on a canal barge moored alongside the building.

Clark's cement plant operation begins at several quarries south of the canal where lime-bearing rock is excavated and loaded in mine cars. When filled, the cars are pulled by horses along a narrow-gauge track across the canal and through the town, arriving at a hill above the cement plant. Here the rock is dumped out and broken up with sledge hammers, then shoveled into kilns where wood has been piled above an iron grate. A fire is lit and the lime cooked for several days, reducing it to a coarse grain. This is shoveled out at the base of the kiln, taken in wheelbarrows to the mill, and ground into cement powder between steam-powered mill stones. The cement is then loaded into barrels and taken away in wagons.

Clark's warehouse is made from blocks of local sandstone, mortared with his cement. Inside, a heavy timber-frame construction supports the floor and ceiling. The building is both a warehouse and a general store, stocking whiskey, coffins, sack grain, and barrels of Clark's cement, among other things. Entrances on either side allow wagons to be driven right through the building for unloading. Sacks of grain and other cargo are loaded on canal barges docked beside the building. The basement of the warehouse contains stalls and mangers for mules.

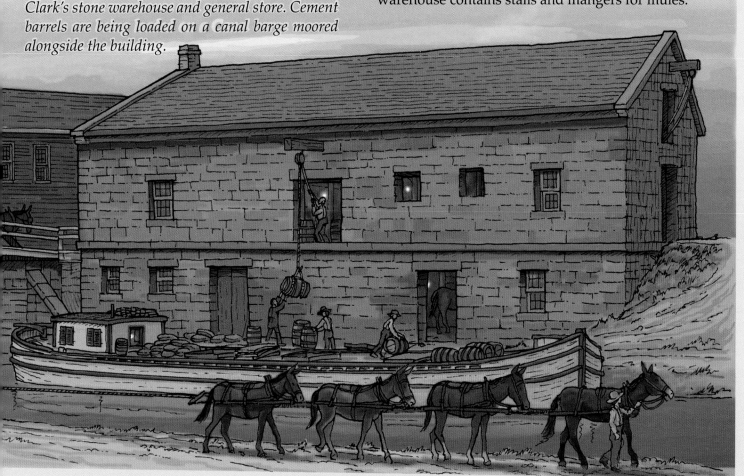

EVENING AT BUFFALO ROCK

Stoking the wood stove and frying up salted pork, johnny cakes, and beans for the evening meal.

Beyond North Utica, darkness settles over the canal bringing with it the cold. This is a region of few habitations, and the only light is from a tin lantern which has been brought out and mounted on the bow. The crew watches carefully for barges and oncoming mule teams in the darkness. In the cabin, Ann readies a meal on the little wood stove, which also provides warmth on a chilly fall evening. Maggie plays with a corn cob doll, beside a table where her father and brother eat a quick meal before returning to the deck. The *Prairie Star* will go as far as Buffalo Rock, before stopping for the night.

Meals often consist of smoked or salted pork, with potatoes, beans, and vegetables making up the rest of the menu. Apples are always a welcomed treat, and sometimes there is fresh food obtained along the way. Drink is usually coffee, or whiskey kept in a jug. Boiling the pork reduces the salty taste, and with a little pork grease in the pan, delicious johnny cakes made from corn meal and buttermilk can be fried up.

The pot and fry pan can get quite greasy and dirty, and the coffee kettle is black and sooty from being kept on the stove. Ashes are put in a bucket and thrown downwind into the canal, so glowing embers don't blow back on deck. Embers can also ignite cloth dresses which is a hazard when cooking on a wood stove. Ann Dawson's work is unending; preparing meals at all hours, cleaning, mending, and looking after the children and their schooling.

When there is time for talk around the cramped cabin table it is usually about tasks needing to be done, although the upcoming presidential election is often a topic these days. The sentiment on this boat is for Lincoln, but there are many Democrats among the Irish population along the canal, so support for Stephen A. Douglas is also strong. Occasionally a fiddle might come out to lighten the mood a little.

Under a rising crescent moon, the *Prairie Star* approaches Buffalo Rock, a large sandstone formation lying between the canal and the Illinois River. This is a lonely stretch, hemmed in by strange rock formations, lakes, and marshes. For the Indians this was once a sacred place, and a big village is said to have stood on the Illinois River just south of here.

The bow lantern provides a dim illumination out into the darkness and the moonlight casts odd shapes on the rocks. Up ahead, the team plods along in the gloom. The mule boy whistles to reassure them, and perhaps himself as well. He has heard talk of how this stretch of the canal is haunted by the spirits of the Indians who once lived around here.

Presently, the canal opens out into a widewater, and the boat can find a safe place to tie-up until morning. The tired mules will be unhitched and tied out at the side of the towpath, to be watered and fed. Once they are secure, everyone can catch a little sleep until first light, when they will start up again.

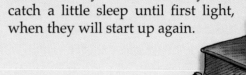

A tin lantern with an oil lamp provides some light for traveling at night.

The boat approaches the widewater and Buffalo Rock in the darkness. In the distance is the light of an oncoming canal barge.

MORNING AT LOCK 12

Arriving at Lock 12 in the early morning, the *Prairie Star* joins several barges waiting to lock through. It may take a while as there is stalled boat traffic in both directions. This is very frustrating for captains trying to keep their boats on schedule. The *Prairie Star* needs to deliver her cargo to the Ottawa public landing this morning, then load corn and be underway again before nightfall. The town is only 3 miles away. The canalers pass time playing cards while the mules pull the boat a little further as each barge locks through.

After more than an hour, most of the traffic has been cleared. A westbound lumber barge locks through followed by its consort, a propeller-driven steam barge. The two will lash together again and then proceed down the canal. Steam barges are a new innovation, and in time they will entirely replace the mule-towed vessels. Most are converted freight boats with crew quarters amidships and boilers and steam engine aft. They are much faster and more efficient, but their greater speed creates wakes that threaten to erode the canal banks, a growing issue for the Canal Commissioners.

Often there are arguments and fights over right-of-way to a lock if two rival boats arrive at the same time. This morning, two mule boys are having an

Canal boats wait their turn at Lock 12 while a steam barge prepares to push a lumber barge.

Lumber barge

argument that quickly degenerates into a fistfight. The *Prairie Star's* mule team is close by and they kick and bray in confusion. This is a dangerous situation that can quickly get out of control and several canalers rush in to calm the animals and stop the fight.

The boat up ahead begins to move as its mule team starts pulling for the lock. Next it will be the *Prairie Star's* turn and she can resume her journey. There's only one more lock to go before she can continue on to the outskirts of Ottawa.

Lock 12

barge

Mule boys in a fistfight, which is quickly broken up before it panics the mule team.

CORN HARVESTING OUTSIDE OTTAWA

Corn shocks

Harvested corn

Corn scythe

Corn horse

Farmers work long hours cutting down corn stalks with scythes, and gathering them up to stack in shocks to dry. A wooden "corn horse" helps support the shock until it is completed.

As the canal nears Ottawa, the bluffs to the north fall away, revealing miles of cornfields in the lands beyond. October is harvest time and the farmers are out in the fields, cutting stalks of corn and stacking them in shocks to dry. Not long ago this was prairie land, but then the canal created a revolutionary new transportation corridor and a steel plow was invented to cut the tough prairie sod.

During the construction of the canal, workers had little use for the scrip they were paid and often used it to purchase land from the grant Congress made to the I&M to raise capital. The canal project attracted land speculators and promoters, and as it neared completion, waves of settlers arrived from the east, lured by the prospect of cheap farm land. In fifteen years, a region of scattered subsistence farms has become an enormous exporter of cash crops. Wheat and oats are raised here, but corn now dominates.

Corn is bulky and difficult to transport. Pioneer farmers would often turn it into whiskey, or use it as feed for hogs, which were easier to get to market. Access to the canal and railroad now make it practical to move corn in bulk to the industrializing cities in the East where demand for food is soaring. Wheat is preferred for flour, but corn makes excellent feed for cattle, hogs, and other animals raised for meat; it also feeds horses and mules and animals of burden.

Harvesting corn is labor intensive. Usually it begins in October or November after other crops have been gathered. Every member of the family and any hired hands work long hours out in the fields, chopping down the stalks with scythes and stacking them in big shocks. After drying a week or so, they return to dig out the ears which are pitched into wagons. Finally the stalks are gathered for animal bedding, and hogs turned loose to glean the fields.

Ears of corn must be shucked by hand to remove the outer casing, another tedious job for the farm family. To help in the task, there are often husking bees where several families and neighbors gather to make the task an enjoyable social occasion.

Once the ears are shucked, they are gathered and shoveled into a rough timber corn crib where they can be stored and dried for months until the farmer needs them for livestock feed or for sale.

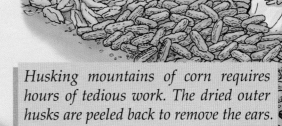

Husking mountains of corn requires hours of tedious work. The dried outer husks are peeled back to remove the ears.

Gaps between the logs of a corn crib allow air to circulate and dry the ears of corn.

Corn is easier to transport and store if it is shelled, which means removing the kernels from a dried cob. In earlier times the farmer might use the edge of a shovel or even have horses tread over the ears. Now there are mechanical shellers making the task easier and faster. Farmers can pay to have their corn shelled in town or do it themselves on the farm. The shelled corn is loaded into sacks or simply shoveled into the bed of a wagon to be taken to a grain elevator.

Two farmhands operate a box-type sheller. A hand-cranked flywheel turns gears and grind wheels inside the wooden box. Corn cobs are fed in at the top and kernels pour out the bottom as the empty cobs are ejected.

OTTAWA AND THE LATERAL CANAL

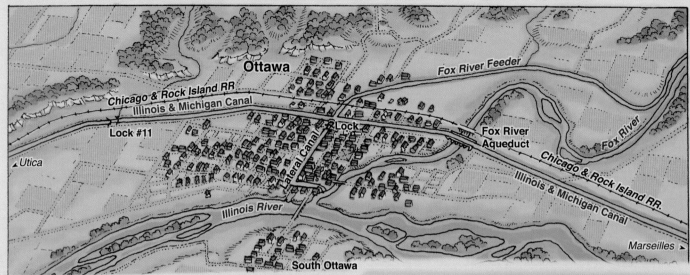

By mid-morning the *Prairie Star* clears Lock 11. The roof-tops and steeples of Ottawa are now visible beneath the glare of a rising sun. At the Fox River Feeder she turns south, nosing under a towpath bridge and entering the lock to the Lateral Canal. Ottawa is the county seat for LaSalle County, and, by 1860, has a population over 9,000. It is a sizable agricultural shipping port and manufacturing center on this section of the canal.

The Lateral Canal is an L-shaped body of water, providing most of the dockage space and hydraulic power for the town. The lock lowers the *Prairie Star* 6 feet and she tows to Ottawa's public landing, passing the I&M Maintenance Yard where tools and materials to repair the canal are stored. South of the public landing are lumberyards and a line of elevating warehouses. At the base of the Lateral Canal is the hydraulic basin where the potential energy of millions of gallons of water is stored. Millraces channel this power to machine shops, flour mills, and sawmills as the water drops 15 feet to the Fox and Illinois Rivers.

Soon after arriving at the public landing, a gang of Irish workers begins muscling the deck cargo ashore. Unloading boats is one of the many laboring jobs available to them and they are sometimes derisively referred to as "Irish power." They haul the heavy molasses barrels out of the hold, while teamster wagons prepare to take them to town. Some will go to a feedlot to be mixed with grain for cattle, the rest to a local brewery to make beer. The millstones will be taken to the City Mills on the Hydraulic Basin.

It takes hours to unload the *Prairie Star* and then the hold must be swept clean and checked for leaks. Captain Dawson walks into town to arrange a cargo of corn, accompanied by his wife Ann who is looking to purchase supplies. Maggie is left in the care of Eric and her brother Charlie, who plays with her in the empty hold, now the safest place on the boat.

William Reddick is an Irish immigrant who has prospered greatly in Ottawa. Orphaned at a young age, he was apprenticed to a glass maker in Ohio. In the 1830s he settled near Ottawa to farm, but then was asked to become the Sheriff of the town. Reddick bought large amounts of land on his salary while land was still cheap, and when the value began to skyrocket, he became a very wealthy man. In 1858, he completed construction of a splendid Italianate mansion across from Lafayette Park.

Reddick Mansion

City Mills

Grinding floor

1) Fox Feeder Canal
2) towpath bridge
3) mill race
4) water power district
5) Lateral Canal lock
6) towpath
7) I&M maintenance yard
8) Ottawa public landing
9) grain elevators
10) Hossack elevator
11) lumber yard
12) feed lot
13) City Mills
14) spillway
15) race gate
16) waterfall
17) business district
18) court house
19) Reddick mansion
20) Lake House
21) toll house
22) swing bridge

In 1860, many small waterpower flour mills are facing competition from steam powered mills in the large cities, however Ottawa's City Mills continues to prosper on the Hydraulic Basin. Grain is hoisted to the top of the building and fed by gravity through spinning millstones on the grinding floor where it is turned into hot meal. It then drops to the floor below to cool and is loaded into barrels as flour.

COURTHOUSE SQUARE

Leaving her husband talking with a forwarding agent, Ann walks down LaSalle Street to a general store where she hopes to find some items she needs on the boat. At Main Street she reaches the magnificent LaSalle County Courthouse, built in 1839 after Ottawa became the county seat. This is the original site of the town and is still its commercial and civic heart.

Ottawa's streets are crowded with meat shops, clothing stores, boot makers, hardware stores, and grocers to mention a few. William Reddick has a dry goods store on Court Street. Ann glances at bonnets in the window of a milliner, as she navigates a wooden sidewalk cluttered with barrels and crates. She crosses dusty streets on narrow plank boards, amidst creaking wagons and whinnying horses. There are many saloons and women usually don't venture here unescorted, but canalers are a tough lot.

The owner of a general store often extends credit to customers or takes produce in exchange, but many go out of business on unpaid debts.

LaSalle and Main Streets at Courthouse Square. Teamsters unload store merchandise from their wagons while lawyers wait outside the courthouse.

Lafayette

CLOTHING

LAH SCHELFE

The general store has dozens of items for sale on cluttered shelves and counters: patent medicines, candles, tinware, cast iron pots and pans, bolts of cloth, utensils, boots, groceries, sacks of flour, and barrels of salt. The wooden floors are stained with tobacco juice. She wants cloth to mend worn clothing and some flour and coffee. She also buys a small slate and chalk to practice sums and letters with the children. Purchases are often on credit or barter. After bargaining with the clerk, she gathers up her purchases and walks out into the beautiful fall afternoon to return to the boat. Several lawyers are discussing a case on a street corner by the courthouse.

Abraham Lincoln, now a candidate for president of the United States, spent several weeks at the courthouse in 1852 serving as a canal commissioner. He heard claims against the State for property damage relating to the building of the I&M Canal. Lincoln is a strong supporter of the canal for the economic benefits it brings, and has traveled by packet boat on several occasions. However, much of his casework now is on behalf of railroad clients.

Two years ago in 1858, Lincoln was in Ottawa again, campaigning for a seat in the United States Senate. It was here that he began a famous series of debates with opponent Judge Stephen A. Douglas, now also a candidate for the presidency. The first debate was held in Lafayette Square, just up LaSalle Street from the courthouse. Although Lincoln ultimately lost the race, the recognition he received ensured his nomination this year as the Republican presidential candidate.

Lincoln Medallion

LaSalle County Courthouse

THE GRAIN ELEVATOR

Grain elevators on the east bank of the Lateral Canal. The Prairie Star is lined up with the spouts.

Once Captain Dawson has secured a cargo for Chicago, he returns to the *Prairie Star* and has her moved down to John Hossack's steam powered grain elevator, one of several on this part of the Lateral Canal. These large wooden buildings are technological marvels in which loading and storing grain has been mechanized so it can be done in enormous volume. Loading a barge at an elevator takes a fraction of the time and labor required to haul and stack grain sacks in a hold. Grain elevators on the I&M handle wheat and oats, but corn predominates.

Corn pours from the spouts into the hold.

Farmers bring their heavily loaded wagons to a ramp beside Hossack's elevator where their corn is graded, weighed, and dumped into a hopper. From here, a steam-powered bucket conveyor raises it, inside a long wooden "leg," up to the head house where the corn is fed into a device with a movable spout called a turn head. A worker in the head house can insert the spout into one of several chutes, each connected to a storage bin of about 10,000 bushels.

Here it is mixed with corn of the exact same grade from other farmers. The bins provide cool, dry storage conditions, free of insects. When the corn is sold, it is emptied by gravity down a spout at the base of the bin into the hold of a waiting canal barge.

The farmer receives a receipt from the elevator owner for the value of his corn according to the market price minus the elevator fee. He can spend it or barter it or deposit it in a bank.

Like many elevator operators, Hossack has grown wealthy as a middleman, giving farmers a reliable way to ship their cash crop to distant markets. The telegraph allows him to monitor market prices in Chicago. But elevating warehouses can be risky ventures. Wooden construction and clouds of grain dust make them vulnerable to explosions and fire. A fire in one elevator can quickly spread to others.

In his private life, Hossack is an ardent abolitionist and his home is a stop on the Underground Railroad. Earlier this year he has been convicted of violating the Fugitive Slave Act for helping captured slave, Jim Gray, escape from an Ottawa courtroom before he could be taken back South.

The *Prairie Star* is maneuvered so her hatches line up with the spouts at the base of the elevator. On a signal from the elevator foreman, the corn flows into her hull in a great golden flood, filling it with over 100 tons in less than an hour. As the corn dust billows up from the hatches, little Maggie and her mother watch from the safety of the cabin.

Captain Dawson receives a bill of lading for the corn; he will be paid for its delivery when he reaches Chicago. A fresh mule team and a new driver are hired and the heavily-loaded boat is towed back to the main line of the I&M Canal. Great care must now be taken to avoid collision, a serious leak could ruin the entire cargo.

Elevating warehouse cutaway illustration

Head house & turn head

Chutes

Storage bins

Steam powered bucket conveyor "leg"

Scale shed

Ramp

Corn

Corn

Spouts

Loading hopper

Loading hopper

Loading hopper

Corn can be moved within the building from storage bins to shipping bins on the canal side of the building.

THE OTTAWA TOLL HOUSE

Before the *Prairie Star* can leave Ottawa, the boat must pay a toll. The collector's office is a small white frame building on the main line of the I&M, just east of the Lateral Canal. Captain Dawson walks up the towpath to the office. Beyond, a low swing bridge across the canal prevents barges going past without paying. Tolls have been collected since the opening of the canal to repay the construction bonds and the cost of operating the waterway. There are tollhouses in LaSalle, Ottawa, Lockport, and Bridgeport.

One toll is charged for the boat and another for its cargo. Captain Dawson must present his bill of lading for the corn to the toll collector who may ask to inspect his boat. Freight boats are charged 2.5 cents per mile, while most goods are charged per thousand pounds per mile. Raw agricultural products such as the *Prairie Star's* corn are charged 3 cents per thousand pounds. Wheat, hay, bran, potatoes, salt, beef, and bales of cotton are charged the same.

Finished products like cheese, butter, sugar, starch, tobacco, and tallow are charged 5 cents. Ale and most liquors are 5 cents, but whiskey is only 3 cents. Grindstones and pig iron are 4 cents, machinery and potters' wares 5 cents, and wagons and vehicles 6 cents. Coal is only 1 cent per thousand pounds and lumber is charged 1.5 cents per thousand board feet.

The office of toll collector is important, and the agent must be honest and reliable. The tollhouse is a simple, one-room building with a desk for documents and reports, a safe for the money collected, and a small wood stove for heat when the weather gets cold. The office is kept open 24 hours with a single clerk to assist the toll collector in his duties.

The toll collector's office and shed on the line of the I&M Canal. A low swing bridge prevents boats from passing by in either direction without paying their tolls.

Presenting the boat's bill of lading to the toll collector for inspection. There will be a toll for both the boat and the cargo it is carrying.

Captain Dawson pays his toll, but still has to wait for several other boats which have come up behind the *Prairie Star* to pay theirs. When everything is in order, the toll collector signals a bridge tender, who slowly cranks open the swing bridge and the boats are free to go. Impatient captains shout to their mule drivers to get the teams underway. Towlines snake through the dirt and then snap taut as the barges slowly begin to move. Wagons and teams on the street will now have to wait for them to pass.

OUTBOUND FOR CHICAGO

Leaving the tollhouse behind, the *Prairie Star* is on her way to Chicago at last. She follows the canal to the outskirts of Ottawa and the Fox River Aqueduct, the most impressive structure on the I&M Canal. On the way there, she passes the Fox River House, a stately old hotel once favored by the packet boats. On the north bank of the canal is an Irish shantytown known as Kerry's Patch.

A few ragged children on the banks of the canal watch the *Prairie Star* as she passes by. The smell of wood cook fires drifts over the water. Kerry Patch, named for County Kerry in Ireland, was one of many shantytowns established during the construction of the canal. Most only lasted through the construction period, but Kerry Patch has remained. Large families pack into small rude dwellings on little plots of land in a narrow tract between the Rock Island Railroad and the canal. Gardens compete with chicken pens and laundry lines for space, as goats and pigs scavenge the rubbish piles.

The Irish often inhabit marginal places on the fringes of towns without proper sanitation or police protection. This leaves many vulnerable to diseases like typhoid and dysentery, and to crime. They are regarded with suspicion and they respond in kind. The Catholic Church is the heart of their community and they have a small parish church, St. Columba, on LaSalle Street near the tollhouse.

Across the canal from Kerry's Patch, an aging wood platform leads back to the Fox River House, established in 1837. In its day, it was one of the finest hotels along the canal, mostly catering to the packet boat trade. This was still the frontier era in Illinois, and taverns and hotels were often quite crude. The Fox River House offered good meals and lodging, and frequently was the social center of Ottawa with dances and balls. Senator Daniel Webster and former president Martin Van Buren have stayed here . With the end of the packet boats, the hotel has fallen on hard times and acquired a dilapidated appearance and reputation.

The I&M Canal narrows as the Prairie Star enters the Fox River Aqueduct which takes the Canal over the Fox River.

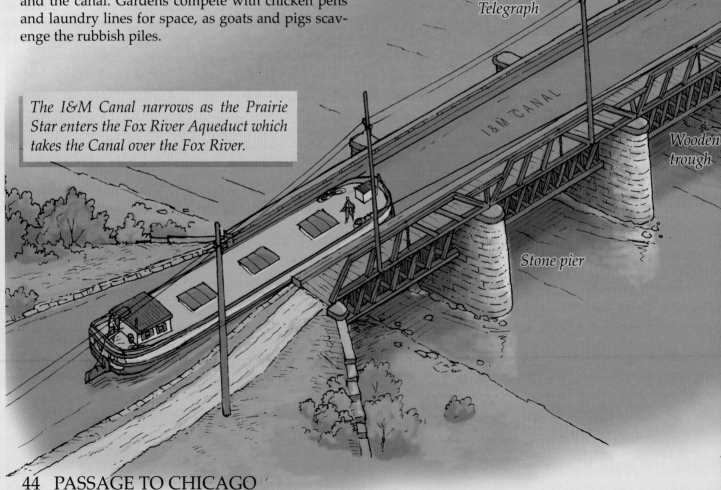

Telegraph

I&M CANAL

Wooden trough

Stone pier

The mules tow the Prairie Star along a wooden platform before they reach the towpath on the other side. The limited space in the trough for water to flow around the boat makes it more difficult for them.

Towpath
bridge

Massive stone piers support a wooden trough that holds 1,600 tons of water suspended above the Fox River.

FOX RIVER

Beyond the Fox River House, the land slopes downward and the canal narrows as it approaches the Fox River Aqueduct. When the I&M was first being planned, one of the main engineering challenges was how to cross the many tributary rivers and creeks that flowed south into the Illinois River. The Fox River was the greatest of these.

The Fox River Aqueduct is 464 feet long and was constructed between 1837 and 1840 by the firm of David Sanger & Sons who had no previous experience building aqueducts. All of the stone was quar-

ried nearby. Seven massive limestone piers and two abutments carry heavy timber trusses supporting a wooden trough with 1,600 tons of water, all suspended above the river. Extensions in the piers hold a wooden platform bridge for the mule teams to cross. The trough is only wide enough for one boat to pass at a time and there isn't much room for water to flow, so the mules have to work even harder to tow the boats across.

Ann allows little Maggie to watch from the cabin window as they enter the aqueduct. The boat seems to float across in mid-air. Below is the disconcerting sound of water leaking out of the wooden trough, one reason that feeder canals are needed to replenish the canal. A louder sound comes over the water from downstream, the roaring of a man-made cascade as water from the hydraulic basin surges down the spillway back to the Fox River.

THE CENTRAL DIVISION

The mule driver leads his team into a broad valley west of Marseilles. About 9,000 years ago, an enormous channel drained the glacial forerunner of the Great Lakes through here.

The mules are a fresh team from a barn in Ottawa, but they are tired from pulling the heavy boat across the aqueduct and their driver Pat has to coax them along the towpath. They are now on the Central Division of the I&M, a region characterized by moraine hills, ancient lake beds, and outwash plains from the recent glacial past. In the next 50 miles from here to Joliet, the *Prairie Star* will gain 40 feet in elevation, requiring five locks. She will cross two more aqueducts at Nettle Creek and Aux Sable, and slack-water basins at the DuPage and Des Plaines Rivers.

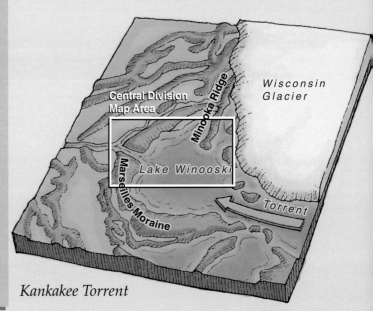

Kankakee Torrent

The towpath travels in a straight line ahead until it vanishes in the distance. A line of hills converges from north and south to form a broad valley. Pat Corcoran is an older mule driver and thinks he has seen everything, but he would be astonished to know what happened here, beginning 20,000 years ago. At that time, this view would have been dominated by an immense wall of ice, the Wisconsin Glacier, forming a barrier across the entire horizon.

A glacier is a river of ice that flows across the land, scouring up debris in its path and carrying it along as glacial till. For thousands of years it advances, until climactic conditions change and the ice retreats by melting back faster than its forward movement. However, the till continues to be pushed forward, so when the glacier pauses in its retreat for a number of years, the till accumulates on its edge as a moraine.

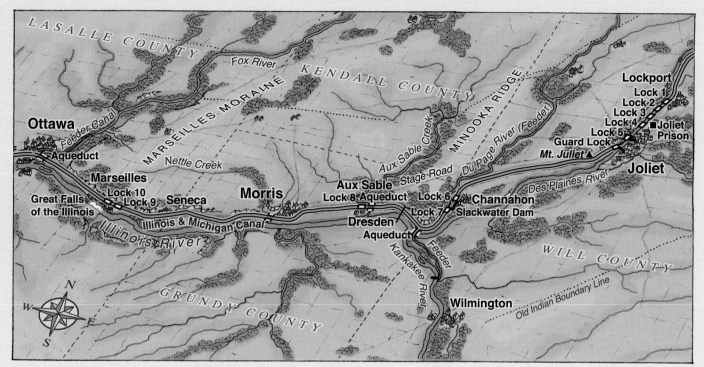

The Central Division
from Ottawa to Joliet

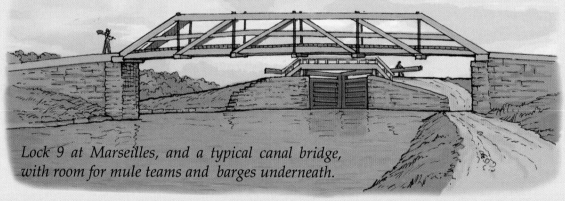

*Lock 9 at Marseilles, and a typical canal bridge,
with room for mule teams and barges underneath.*

When the Wisconsin Glacier retreated from here 20,000 years ago it left the Marseilles Moraine and behind it, the glacial meltwater formed Lake Wauponsee. Over a thousand years the lake slowly drained away while the Wisconsin Glacier continued its retreat. Then, 16,000 years ago, a catastrophic flood was released from the Great Lakes, known as the Kankakee Torrent. In as little as three weeks, the ancient lake bed was refilled and then broke through the Marseilles Moraine at this place releasing a tremendous cascade. The powerful flood scoured and gouged out the valley from here to LaSalle and beyond. The torrent was strong enough to force the Mississippi River out of its former bed in the Illinois Valley and into its present course, further west.

By late afternoon, the Prairie Star has reached Marseilles. Pat coaxes the team towards a set of locks up ahead. The canal is confined within a valley whose weathered bluffs once witnessed a flood of unimaginable power. Locks 10 and 9 are only a few hundred yards apart and raise the canal over a 16-foot change in elevation, all that remains of an ancient waterfall. A two-mile stretch of rapids on the Illinois River to the south is another remnant. Known as the Great Falls, it was one of the obstacles to river navigation that required the I&M Canal.

Although it is an excellent location for waterpower, Marseilles has not been able to take much advantage of it as yet and the village is still quite small in 1860.

THE VALLEY OF THE ILLINOIS

At sunset, the boat is three miles past Lock 9, where the canal leaves the Marseilles Moraine behind and the Illinois Valley opens out into a broad plain once again. The fall colors on the hillside and the golden hue of the cornfields fade into darkness. The bottomlands are part of the ancient basin of Lake Wauponsee which over thousands of years has transformed from meltwater lake, to marsh, to prairie, and now, rich agricultural land.

Ahead is the village of Seneca, a small grain port with a single elevator on the canal and another planned for next year (this second elevator will be the last of its kind along the I&M Canal). The *Prairie Star* has 9 miles to go to Morris, where Captain Dawson hopes to tie up briefly for the night. First however, he must hire a fresh team and driver from a mule barn in Seneca. He needs to deliver his bulk corn to an elevator in Chicago on schedule and then arrange for another cargo. The cold evenings remind him the I&M will be closing for the season soon.

MARSEILLES MORAINE

Old Stage Road

Chicago Rock Island R.R.

I&M CANAL

Morris

Seneca

ILLINOIS RIVER

LUMBERYARDS AT MORRIS

Grundy County Courthouse

Cooper wagon

Yard office

County Jail

Lumber wagon

Early in the morning, the *Prairie Star* is on the Morris widewater, after stopping for the night west of town. Morris is the county seat of Grundy County, and the largest town on this part of the I&M. Along the banks of its widewater are warehouses, blacksmith shops, cooper shops and other enterprises including several lumberyards. South of the canal are feedlots, and the bellowing of cattle joins the braying of mules this morning.

At the lumber yard, a couple of barges are being unloaded. Men clamber on top of the nearest boat while others take up positions on lumber stacks in the yard. Morris has a large Irish population, along with German and Canadian immigrants, and lumber shoving is a job often available to them.

Lumber is a common cargo on the canal, since northern Illinois is mostly prairie and construction timber is scarce. Much of it is white pine from Michi-

Along Canal Street in Morris, farmers and builders load their wagons while lumber shovers move board pine from the barges to stacks in the yard.

White Pine

MICHIGAN

WHITE PINE

WISCONSIN

LAKE

White Pine

Lumber

MICHIGAN

Lumber

Chicago

ILLINOIS

Illinois & Michigan Canal

Illinois River

INDIANA

Illinois River

Livestock pens and feed lots

Morris Widewater

Lumber barges

I&M CANAL

Lumber yard

Cooper shop

Lumber wagon

gan and Wisconsin. Trees are harvested in winter and floated to sawmills in the spring to be cut into boards and shipped on schooners to Chicago, the greatest lumber market in the world. The boards are graded and stacked in yards to season until loaded on canal barges and rail cars. I&M captains are always looking for return cargos from Chicago, so shipping rates are cheap. Pine is straight and clean and easy to work; it is ideal for a revolutionary new method of construction known as balloon framing. A skeleton of boards held together with nails can be quickly erected without needing skilled carpenters.

The lumber shovers move boards from the barges across to men on the lumber stacks. The wood must be sorted and stacked in the yard, with high quality boards for furniture or clapboard finishing in one area, and lower-quality material for farm structures and humble dwellings in another. This is bruising work and must be done quickly. Some boats carry shingles for roofs or wood for fence posts, even bark for tanning. Farmers and builders, coopers, wagon shops and tool makers are all customers at the yard.

Leaving Morris, the *Prairie Star* stops at a mule barn on the east side of town for a fresh team. Jack Mack, a resident of Morris, owns hundreds of mules and employs scores of mule drivers. He operates mule barns every 12 miles from here to Chicago.

ALONG THE OLD STAGE ROAD

From LaSalle-Peru to Joliet, the I&M Canal shares the Illinois River valley with a more ancient transportation route, the Great Sauk Trail. For centuries the trail was used by Native American tribes for communication and trade. In the 1830s, portions of it became a road for settlers moving west and stage coaches traveling from Chicago to LaSalle. With the passing of the frontier and the end of the stage lines, the Old Stage Road as it is now called, is just another country track. This morning the travelers are a couple of drovers, a big farm dog, and a herd of pigs they are taking to a feedlot in Morris.

Just outside Morris, the stage road passes a little cemetery where last year old Chief Shabbona was buried, a sign of the vanishing frontier. In the War of 1812, he fought for the British alongside Tecumseh,

Drovers herd pigs on the old stage road, shouting "soo-eey, soo-eey," to keep them going. The pigs don't need much encouragement; they want to wallow in the little stream up ahead.

but later, became convinced of the futility of opposing the Americans. During the Black Hawk War of 1832, he warned settlers of Sauk raids, earning their gratitude, but in the end it didn't do him much good. When the Potawatomis were forced by treaty to sign away their lands, making the construction of the I&M Canal possible, Shabbona had to move with them across the Mississippi. Eventually he was able to return to live out his final years near Morris.

When the pigs reach Morris they will be fattened on corn for several days before going to a stockyard in Chicago. Prior to the canal, farmers had to drive their livestock there on primitive roads. Animals lost weight on the way, particularly the hogs. Once the canal was opened, farmers could slaughter them and pack the salted meat in barrels to put on barges. Now animals are herded live on to rail cars at a depot.

During the frontier period, the stage road crossed the Aux Sable Creek at a rocky ford a half mile above its confluence with the Illinois River. Later a sawmill was established a little further up the creek. When the canal came through, a lock and aqueduct were built in 1847 with stone quarried very near the site.

Irish immigrants provided most of the labor, some hired right off the boat. They lived in squalid conditions and suffered from typhoid outbreaks and dysentery. Some refused to work in summer unless given whiskey, which they believed would protect them from malaria. In 1849, a cholera epidemic reached the canal, resulting in hundreds of deaths. When the Aux Sable section of the canal was completed, most of the Irish moved on, abandoning their shantytown which gradually returned to the soil.

Once the canal was opened and the packet boats began scheduled runs, Aux Sable became a lively little village, attracting a saloon and a general store for passengers waiting at the lock. There was even a dentist and a tailor and a

distillery by the ford. However, with the demise of the packet boats and the overland stage lines in the 1850s, the merchants left for Morris and Aux Sable became a quiet backwater once again.

As the *Prairie Star* comes within hailing distance of Lock 8, Captain Dawson blows his boat horn and calls out "lock-ee," but the locktender is already busy with another barge, so he must wait. His wife Ann takes the opportunity to get off the boat with Maggie to visit the locktender's family.

Lock 8 and the aqueduct at Aux Sable Creek. A barge locks through while the Prairie Star waits by the bank.

Aqueduct

Aux Sable Creek

Ford

Farm House

Distillery

Lock tender's house and gardens

Lock 8

I & M CANAL

Old Stage Road

LOCKTENDERS AT AUX SABLE

The locktender at Aux Sable is an employee of the canal, and reports to the superintendent of the Central Division. His main responsibility is the smooth and safe operation of Lock 8, and for this he receives a small salary and free lodging for his family in a house by the lock.

A locktender on the I&M works 18 hours a day and is on call 24 hours. The lock machinery can be difficult to operate, particularly the heavy gates, and balance beams are needed to swing them open and shut. On days when 30 or more boats come through, the work can be exhausting. If only one locktender is available, he may have to cross the balance beams using an iron railing to reach the gates on the other side. He has to be careful not to fall into the lock chamber and risk drowning. Usually a locktender has an assistant or a family member to help, which may be his wife, or even a daughter.

The locktender must answer the bargeman's horn in any kind of weather, from heavy thunderstorms, to sleet and hail. He often has to deal with impatient captains and settle arguments, even break up fights, over right-of-way. He has to be watchful at all hours. It is not unknown for boat crews to try and lock themselves through late at night, rather than waiting for a locktender to rouse himself from his bed. A seriously damaged lock gate can close an entire section of the canal for days.

As each boat passes through, the locktender is required to check the cargo manifest and make sure the tolls have been paid. When he has time he clears weeds and debris near the lock gates, repairs any damage to equipment, and maintains nearby canal culverts and weirs. He also checks the water levels on either side of the lock. A drop might indicate a serious leak or a millrace using too much water.

He receives less than a dollar per day for his work, a wage that makes it hard to support a family, even with free lodging. Often family members must find other jobs and maintain gardens to sell or barter produce to passing boats. They mend clothing, do wash, even cook meals to earn extra income.

The locktender's house is a two-story frame building, measuring 18 by 25 feet. The canal commissioners had it built in 1848, in simple Greek Revival style with clapboard siding, and it is much like every other locktender's house on the canal. There is a sitting room and kitchen on the main floor, and two bedrooms upstairs. If the locktender has a large family there isn't much room or privacy. Boats and mule teams pass by all day and night and the locktender and his family have come to know most of the canalers very well.

Ann Dawson walks with Maggie up the towpath to the house, to see if she can barter some of the cloth she obtained in Ottawa. She has just enough time to trade for some vegetables and potatoes, fresh eggs, and a loaf of bread. She hurriedly exchanges news with the family and offers greetings to relatives, as the boat rises in the lock. Then, boosting little Maggie to Charlie, she steps back on board as the mules pull in their harnesses and the *Prairie Star* begins to move out of the lock.

DRESDEN, PAPER TOWN

MINOOKA RIDGE

Stage Road

Cemetery

Rutherford Barn

Rutherford Tavern

Illinois & Michigan Canal

Illinois River

A mile and a half past Aux Sable the boat comes in sight of the Minooka Ridge, a 25 mile long moraine running north to south that once formed the eastern boundary of ancient Lake Winooski. Ahead is a large wooden barn perched on the canal berm, and beside it a barge is loading sacks of grain while several mules are led out to pasture. The barn is part of Dresden, a village that once seemed destined to become a great port on the canal.

Salmon Rutherford settled here in 1834, establishing a tavern and a stage line. Horses could be changed here and weary travelers might enjoy a meal or spend the night. The following year another tavern was built, and with planning underway for the canal, prospects for a town looked bright. Rutherford had a plat made for a city of 63 blocks, and settlers and businesses began to be attracted to the area. The barn alongside the canal was built as a warehouse for loading grain on passing barges. It also contained a small number of stalls for mules. Unfortunately, when the railroad bypassed the village to the north it spelled the end of Rutherford's dream and Dresden became one more "paper" town.

Past the barn, the I&M converges on the Minooka Ridge, hugging its southern flank and hemmed in by the Illinois River, before vanishing behind the ridge on the way to Channahon. Nearby, the Illinois River divides into two main branches: the Kankakee, flowing up from the south, and the Des Plaines, which the canal now follows to the northeast. The Kankakee supplies water to the canal from a feeder channel that begins near Wilmington and crosses over the Des Plaines River via a 400-foot long aqueduct.

Aqueduct
Kankakee Feeder
Des Plaines R.
Kankakee R.

Passing a couple of lumber barges. There are strict rules governing right-of-way when boats pass each other on the canal.

Following the curve of the canal around the southern tip of Minooka Ridge, a couple of lumber barges unexpectedly appear from behind the hill, traveling in the opposite direction. Great care must be taken to avoid entangling the teams; there are strict rules on the canal for vessels needing to pass each other.

The *Prairie Star* is pulling against the current and has the right-of-way, so the closer lumber boat halts its team and lets the towline sink to the bottom of the canal. It steers to the opposite bank, giving the *Prairie Star* room to pass, while its mule team moves aside on the towpath, allowing the *Prairie Star's* mules to go by. The big animals nimbly step over the lumber barge's towrope and the boats begin to pass.

However, the space to get around the other boat is limited and the *Prairie Star* deals her a glancing blow to the stern, which brings forth a storm of curses. This is a pretty common occurrence on the canal and the bumpers cushion most of the shock, but the hold will have to be checked. Any leaks could be ruinous.

CHANNAHON AND THE DUPAGE RIVER

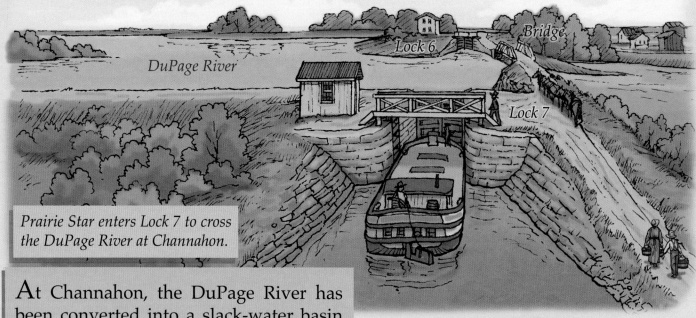

DuPage River

Lock 6

Bridge

Lock 7

Prairie Star enters Lock 7 to cross the DuPage River at Channahon.

At Channahon, the DuPage River has been converted into a slack-water basin for barges to cross. A dam downstream increases the depth of the river, allowing them to float from Lock 7 to Lock 6 along a timber crib spillway next to a towpath bridge. Lock 7 raises the boats 4 feet to the basin, and Lock 6 raises them another 8 feet to a canal level that takes them 10 miles to a guard lock at Joliet, and a set of basins on the Des Plaines.

William Gooding opted for a slack-water dam here rather than building another expensive aqueduct. The basin also provides hydraulic power for Channahon which can be leased. And the dam allows the river to supply water to the I&M as a feeder.

The DuPage is one of four main feeders, along with the Fox, Kankakee, and Sag Channel. There is also a pumping station on the Chicago River. The DuPage has a watershed surface of about 500 square miles. A channel north of Lock 6 taps into the watershed which is fed to the canal by a control gate that regulates the flow. The lock-tender at Channahon is responsible for the gate and maintaining proper depth in the canal. There is often insufficient water in dry periods which is a chronic problem for the I&M. Barges are often forced to carry reduced cargos or risk grounding.

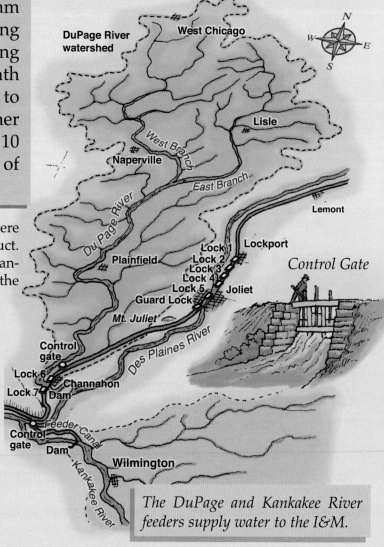

DuPage River watershed

West Chicago

Lisle

West Branch

Naperville

East Branch

Lemont

DuPage River

Lockport

Lock 1
Lock 2
Lock 3
Lock 4
Lock 5

Plainfield

Control Gate

Joliet

Guard Lock

Mt. Juliet

Des Plaines River

Control gate

Lock 6

Channahon

Lock 7

Dam

Control gate

Dam

Feeder Canal

Kankakee River

Wilmington

The DuPage and Kankakee River feeders supply water to the I&M.

Today is wash day. Ann and her son Charlie get off the boat before Lock 7 and walk up the towpath to fill buckets from the cleaner flowing water by the spillway. Water from the canal is often foul and unsuitable. They reboard the boat at Lock 6, and take the buckets into the cabin for Ann to heat the wash water on the wood stove. While she is doing this, the *Prairie Star* changes mule teams at a barn near Channahon for the 10-mile tow to Joliet.

Many working boats on the canal can be quite dirty. Since this one is managed by a family, the decks are swept and clothes and bedding kept clean. This is hard work, the laundry is scrubbed on a washboard in a wooden tub with soap made of wood ash lye and animal lard. The soap is caustic and hands are soon rubbed raw. Maggie watches her mother scrubbing clothes, safely tethered to a line to keep her from falling into the canal. She gets a scolding for sucking her thumb. Her father Henry will rig up a clothesline so the wash can be hung up to dry. But first he opens the hatches and checks the hold once more for leaks, following the boat's recent collision.

Later in the afternoon the boat passes Mount Juliet, where chimney smoke can be seen rising from Joliet just over the horizon. Mount Juliet is a large mound of gravel and clay deposited by the Wisconsin Glacier. An important site for native peoples, and much remarked upon by European travelers from as far back as Marquette and Joliet, now the mound is being excavated away for clay to make drainage tiles. In another decade this interesting natural feature will completely vanish from the landscape.

Wash day on the boat.

Examining hold for leaks.

Passing Mount Juliet with the wash hung up to dry. Joliet is two miles distant on the horizon.

JOLIET, RAILROADS

Passing under the Chicago & Rock Island railway bridge on the way into Joliet.

Coal yard

Entering Joliet, Ann takes in the clothes that are drying on a line before the boat reaches the Chicago & Rock Island railway bridge where steam trains pass overhead amid clouds of sooty, acrid-smelling smoke. Joliet's early growth owes much to the canal and to a wealth of limestone discovered during the canal construction. With the arrival of the railroad, Joliet has come into its own as an industrial city, and now only Chicago is larger.

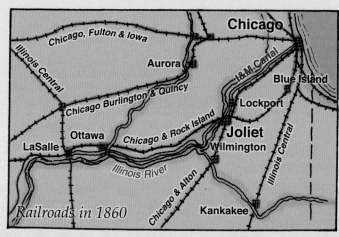

Railroads in 1860

Like many towns along the canal, Joliet is only about 25 years old. First settled in the aftermath of the Black Hawk War, it was a fairly typical frontier town. However, with the canal construction and the discovery of limestone deposits in the region, Joliet came to supply most of the building stone for the I&M's locks, aqueducts, and culverts. It was known as "stone city" and its particular variety of Joliet limestone, a bluish-yellowish stone, grew in demand once it could be shipped out on canal barges. Joliet also benefited from the flow of the Des Plaines River in this place, with numerous mills and other waterpower-based industries established.

Joliet's citizens lobbied for railroads, influenced by the success of Chicago, which was sending rail lines out into the hinterlands and capturing much of the agricultural trade. Railroads could be built anywhere and at less expense than canals. Railroads were faster and captured time-sensitive cargoes such as livestock, merchandise, and passenger traffic. Trains ran on set schedules year-round, unlike canals that closed in the winter.

In 1852, the Chicago, Rock Island & Pacific Railway came to Joliet, and by 1853, the line was completed to LaSalle paralleling the Illinois & Michigan Canal for most of the way. In 1855, Joliet added the Chicago & Alton Railroad, as the city was fast becoming a rail center second only to Chicago. Railroads spurred industrial development such as rolling mills which were needed to make steel rails. Locomotive repair shops created new kinds of jobs for skilled workers.

The I&M Canal remained competitive with the railroad by concentrating on bulk cargoes, which also helped to keep the rail rates down. Industries in the rapidly expanding city still relied on canal boats to carry coal, lumber, and stone along with agricultural products that continued shipping on the canal.

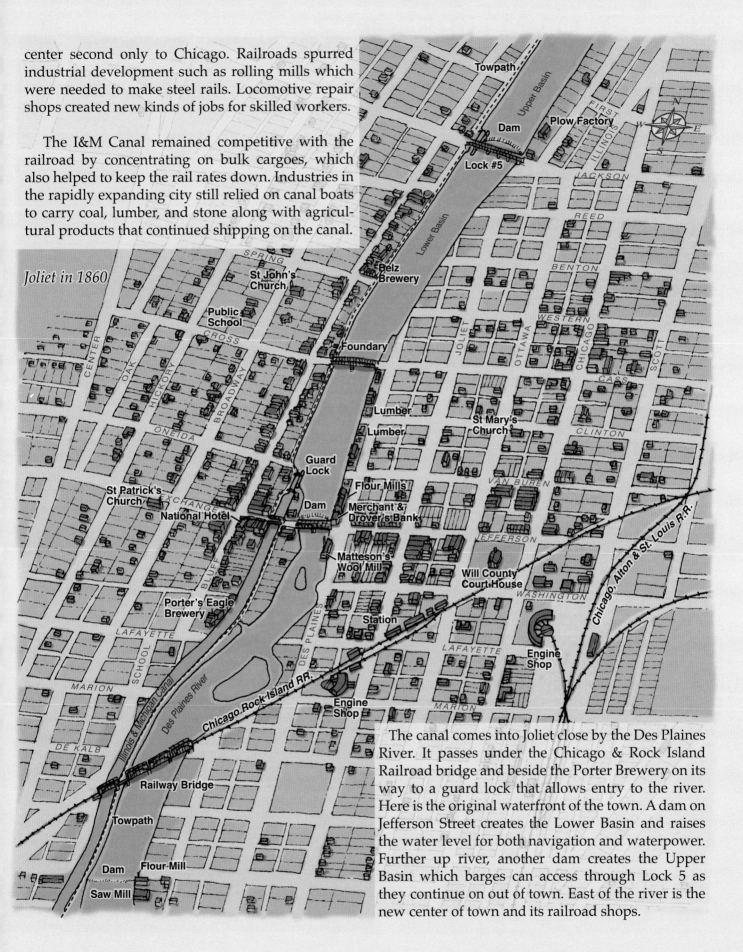

Joliet in 1860

The canal comes into Joliet close by the Des Plaines River. It passes under the Chicago & Rock Island Railroad bridge and beside the Porter Brewery on its way to a guard lock that allows entry to the river. Here is the original waterfront of the town. A dam on Jefferson Street creates the Lower Basin and raises the water level for both navigation and waterpower. Further up river, another dam creates the Upper Basin which barges can access through Lock 5 as they continue on out of town. East of the river is the new center of town and its railroad shops.

THE OLD WATERFRONT

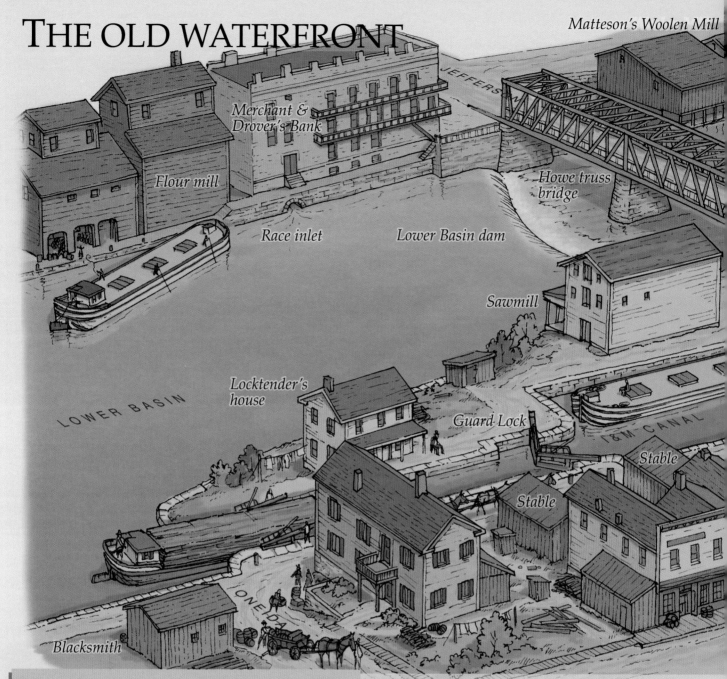

Matteson's Woolen Mill

Merchant & Drover's Bank

Flour mill

JEFFERSON

Howe truss bridge

Race inlet

Lower Basin dam

Sawmill

Locktender's house

Guard Lock

LOWER BASIN

I&M CANAL

Stable

Stable

ONE DA

Blacksmith

By early-afternoon, the *Prairie Star* has reached the guard lock that connects the canal with the Lower Basin of the Des Plaines River. This area is Joliet's original waterfront, dating to a time when commerce was dominated by the I&M. The tired mules plod up a ramp to a change-over bridge on Exchange Street which will take them across to the towpath on the other side. The bowsman casts off the towline and the boat glides underneath.

The guard lock protects the canal from high water, while allowing access to the Lower Basin. The large semicircular dam above Jefferson Street forms the Lower Basin and provides water power for several flour mills on the east bank. Canal boats can be poled across to load cargo, but need be careful of the current or risk being swept over the dam.

The old waterfront is still a lively place. Where the towpath descends to the guard lock, is the Omnibus block, a two-story frame building with a saloon, meat market, and general store. Here it is said a bargeman can order groceries, get a good cut of meat and have a drink, all before his boat clears the lock.

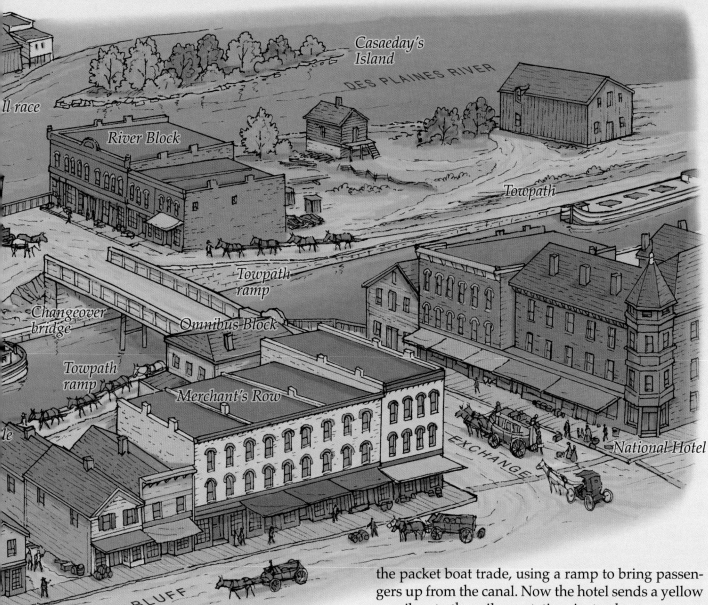

Casaeday's Island

DES PLAINES RIVER

River Block

ll race

Towpath

Towpath ramp

Changeover bridge

Omnibus Block

Towpath ramp

Merchant's Row

EXCHANGE

National Hotel

le

BLUFF

Beside the Jefferson Street bridge is the abandoned woolen mill of Joel A. Matteson, governor of Illinois from 1853 to 1857. Matteson was a contractor for the I&M before opening the mill, Joliet's first important manufacturing industry. He wields political influence in legislative districts all along the canal, but his reputation has been tarnished recently by $200,000 of missing canal scrip found in his possession.

Overlooking the old waterfront is Bluff Street, lined with stores and businesses and busy with wagon traffic. Most of these have turned their back on the canal, relying on the railroad to supply merchandise. The waterfront is now avoided by most pedestrians on the streets above. At Bluff and Exchange is Merchants Row, and across the street is the National Hotel, a business that has made the transition from canal to railroad. In an earlier day, the hotel relied on the packet boat trade, using a ramp to bring passengers up from the canal. Now the hotel sends a yellow omnibus to the railway station, instead.

The *Prairie Star's* sweating mule team reaches the crossover bridge on its way to the guard lock. The driver whistles and shouts to the braying mules to keep them moving. He briefly shares Exchange Street with the foot traffic, much to their dismay.

Once through the guard lock, the *Prairie Star* tows up the west bank, headed for Lock 5 and the Upper Basin. Here the waterfront was once populated with livery stables, saloons, and boarding houses, but it looks a little deserted now. Dawson hires another team and driver, the sixth since the trip began. The neighborhood is mostly made up of German immigrants. Joliet has developed several breweries since their arrival in the 1840s, beginning with the Belz Brewery just off the towpath. The east side makes whiskey; the west side makes beer.

CLIMBING TO LOCKPORT

Crossing the Des Plaines River back into the canal.

Once past Lock 5, the *Prairie Star* passes several abandoned stone quarries, dating to the original construction of the canal. Outside Joliet, the towpath follows a long earthen embankment to a wooden bridge that takes it across the Des Plaines River. Captain Dawson braces his feet against the deck cleats and holds the tiller in position to fight the current and keep the boat to the center of the channel. He tries to avoid putting too much strain on the mule team up on the bridge. After the bridge, a series of four locks will raise the *Prairie Star* 40 feet to Lockport. The town is only two miles away, but the boat will spend several hours getting there.

To reach Lockport, the canal climbs 40 feet out of the Des Plaines River valley, using four locks in about two miles, the greatest elevation change on the waterway.

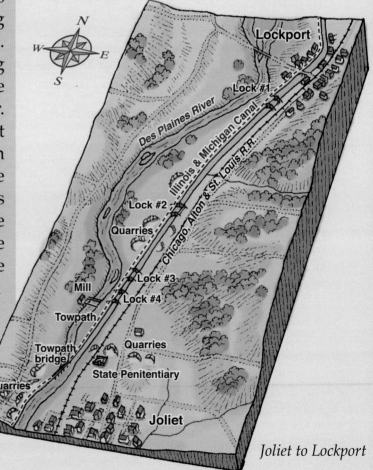

Joliet to Lockport

The newly-built Joliet Penitentiary.

Beyond the crossing of the Des Plaines River, the canal borders the newly completed Joliet State Penitentiary. The state legislature authorized this location in 1857, and contracted Lorenzo Sanger and Samuel Casey to build the prison using limestone from a pit north of the site and convict labor from an overcrowded prison in Alton. The penitentiary opened in June 1860 and is distinctively medieval in appearance, but it is designed and run according to the most modern and humane principles. Prisoners in striped uniforms and under guard work just across the canal as the mules walk past. The driver takes care to keep out of sight behind the team.

At Lock 4, the *Prairie Star* begins her climb to the Lockport Basin, passing more quarries on the west side of the canal. There isn't much traffic and she is able to reach Lock 1 before sunset. Ahead is the Norton warehouse and beyond that, the Lockport Public Landing. Chicago is 29 miles away. It has been two and a half days days since leaving LaSalle, and after one more brief stop for the night, the *Prairie Star* should be on the Chicago River tomorrow afternoon.

Lock 1 and the Lockport Basin.

In the original plan for the I&M, Lock 1 was to be the first, with the canal dug below the level of Lake Michigan all the way to Lockport from Chicago. When this "deep cut" plan proved too expensive, two additional locks were needed to raise the first section of the canal above a ridge at Summit. Three locktenders reside in Lockport and they are responsible for all four locks from the penitentiary to here.

NORTON AND COMPANY

Hiram Norton's steam-powered warehouse in Lockport is one of the largest and most substantially built on the canal. It has storage capacity for 50,000 bushels of corn. Wagons line up in front of a small scale building to be weighed and enter the warehouse through a set of arched doors to unload. During the harvest, hundreds of wagons may arrive each day.

Norton came to Lockport from Canada in 1838 and opened a general store on the landing. He immediately realized the potential for forwarding bulk grain to Chicago and was soon moving loaded wagons up Archer Avenue and returning with merchandise for his store. With the opening of the canal, his business soared. Lockport is the last large transfer point for grain and other agricultural products on the canal before Chicago. Norton built his warehouse in 1848 and now owns several mills and warehouses in Lockport. Like John Hossack in Ottawa, Hiram Norton is also an ardent abolitionist.

Farmers are given a credit slip for their corn and wheat which are elevated within the building by a steam-powered bucket and conveyor system. Barges on the canal side can be unloaded by steam-power as well. The warehouse also mills corn into cornmeal, using grindstones on the first floor, and shells corn for a fee. Norton even offers free accommodation for customers and their teams overnight when needed.

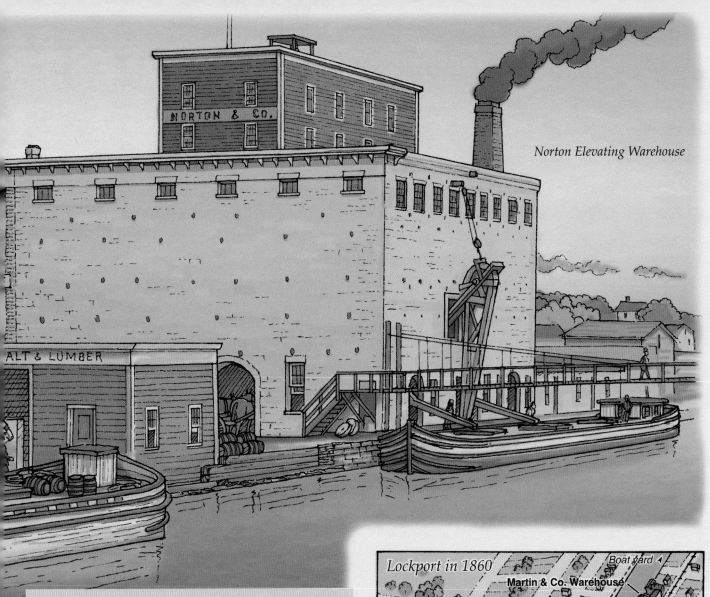

Norton Elevating Warehouse

NORTON & CO.

ALT & LUMBER

Wagons enter the scale house to be weighed while a barge is unloaded on the canal side of the building.

A three-story addition on the east side of the building has office space and a general store. Here farmers can exchange their credit slips for an equal value of goods. The store also stocks boat supplies where canalers can purchase rope and lanterns and other equipment needed for their barges. Norton operates his own barges between Lockport and Chicago.

In 1848, the canal commissioners contracted George Barnett to excavate a 370 by 260 foot hydraulic basin off the main line of the canal. The leasing of hydraulic power is an important revenue source for the canal along with tolls and cutting ice in winter. Lockport is one of the most promising locations, with a 21 foot fall of water to the Des Plaines River. The potential could have been greater under the original "deep cut" plan; however, the basin's

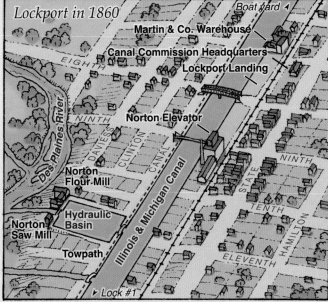

Lockport in 1860

Boat Yard
Martin & Co. Warehouse
Canal Commission Headquarters
Lockport Landing
Norton Elevator
Norton Flour Mill
Hydraulic Basin
Norton Saw Mill
Towpath
Lock #1
Des Plaines River
EIGHTH
NINTH
DAVIESS
CLINTON
CANAL
Illinois & Michigan Canal
STATE
NINTH
TENTH
HAMILTON
ELEVENTH

hydraulic power was more than sufficient. Soon after it was completed, Norton negotiated sole rights to the hydraulic basin for a sawmill and a flour mill. Barges enter from the canal under a towpath bridge and load flour barrels by the mill.

THE PUBLIC LANDING

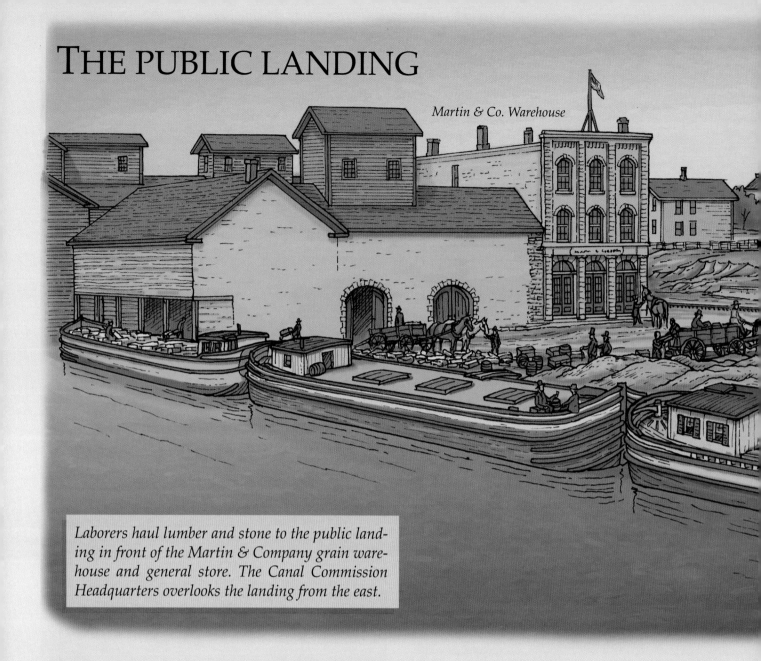

Martin & Co. Warehouse

Laborers haul lumber and stone to the public landing in front of the Martin & Company grain warehouse and general store. The Canal Commission Headquarters overlooks the landing from the east.

A few hundred feet past Norton's warehouse is the Lockport Public Landing. Here a line of canal barges is unloading building materials as the day comes to a close. Since most canal frontage is privately owned, towns usually have a public landing where citizens can freely exchange goods with barges on the canal. A builder has arranged for lumber to be shipped to the landing directly from a yard on the Chicago River along with stone from a quarry near Lemont.

In the early years of the canal, a farmer might bring his wagon to the landing and load sacks of grain directly on a boat or arrange for lumber to be shipped from a yard in Chicago. Sugar, molasses, and other goods from the South were unloaded here along with manufactured items from the East. However, as the canal has shifted to bulk cargo, public landings are being used less frequently in this way.

Bordering the north side of the landing is the warehouse and store of Colonel George Martin, a local Lockport grain merchant. This building was originally constructed by the canal commissioners in 1838 to store equipment and materials being used in the construction of the canal. Martin purchased it after the canal was completed and converted it into a

Canal Commission Headquarters

Chicago, Alton & St. Louis R.R.

Lockport Landing

grain warehouse. He has added grain bins and a head house in addition to making other improvements. Just last year he demolished part of the warehouse and contracted a German immigrant, Julius Scheibe, to build a beautiful 3-story Italianate addition for use as an office space and general store. Martin also owns several other grain elevators.

Up on the hill overlooking the public landing is the old canal headquarters building, established by the Commissioners in 1837, and still serving that role in 1860. The building houses important documents relating to the canal, along with several resident canal engineers. It has a safe to hold monies to pay workers and contractors, as well as receipts from the toll houses. William Gooding located the headquar-

ters in Lockport because of its excellent waterpower potential, which he was convinced would be essential to the success of the canal. This decision led to a lot of grumbling from the citizens of Joliet and there is still a strong rivaly between the two towns.

The tracks for the Chicago, Alton & St. Louis Railroad borders the eastern side of the landing. The line arrived in Lockport in 1858, and steam trains pass frequently on their way to and from Chicago. Four and a half years from now this place will be crowded with people wishing to pay their last respects to Abraham Lincoln, as his funeral train travels down this same line on the final leg of its journey to Springfield. By then the I&M will have seen some of its busiest years in the service of the Union war effort.

THE LOCKPORT BOAT YARD

The glow of the setting sun illuminates a barge under construction at the Lockport Boat Yard, as the *Prairie Star* goes past. When the I&M first opened, only 16 boats were available. Many short-lived yards appeared to fill the gap, including one on the Lockport Landing. In 1854, O.D. Brooks received permission from the town and the commissioners for a permanent yard at 4th Street and the canal. It is now one of three boat yards on the canal; the others are in Chicago and Peru.

The yard keeps busy building and repairing boats. The *Joliet Signal* reported in 1856 that 15 boats were built in the last season with 9 more under construction. The yard employs carpenters and boat builders and a blacksmith to forge iron fittings. There is a large warehouse for storing timbers and manufacturing oakum to caulk seams.

The boat hulls are framed and planked in white oak, which is strong and durable. The decks are planked in white pine which is easily obtained from Chicago lumber yards. During winter, local farmers can be employed to haul timber to the yard for extra income. The barges are made ready to launch by the opening of the navigation season in March or April.

To begin construction, a large section of level ground is selected next to the canal bank. Boats are

Driving lines of oakum into the seams between planks to make them watertight.

Shaping timbers with an adze and sawing planks with a whipsaw.

launched sideways into the water. First, keel blocks are laid out for the length of the vessel and then a keel plank laid on top. Curved timbers are made by bending planks over steaming cauldrons until the wood holds its shape. The hull frames are slid into position about a foot apart, raised and fastened to the keel plank. When the frames are all in place, the bow and stern sections are built. Finally, the planking is nailed in place and lengths of oakum (cotton rolled in tar) is pounded into the seams between planks to make the hull watertight.

The carpenters are skilled craftsmen and supply their own tools. Curved adzes are used to shape timbers and smooth the hull form. Men cut planks with whipsaws, one man standing on top of a platform and another below. Caulkers with wooden mallets and caulking irons drive oakum into seams.

Wooden boats last 15 to 25 years. Once the timbers start to rot, a canal boat will require frequent repair and caulking and must be winched sideways out of the canal at the yard. When beyond repair, barges are often used as breakwaters or sunk in Lake Michigan or simply abandoned after any useful fittings are removed.

The yard looks chaotic with cut timbers lying everywhere, but the boat builders are masters of their craft learned from years of experience.

THE SUMMIT DIVISION

Lemont

The canal approaching Lemont.

Three miles north of Lockport, the canal begins a broad curve to the east, following the Des Plaines River. It is dark now, and Eric Lindgren has mounted the boat's lantern which dimly illuminates the water ahead. The only other light is from a southbound train to Joliet. Ahead the canal enters another ancient drainage valley through a glacial moraine. Here, beds of exposed limestone have attracted quarries and immigrant labor to the town of Lemont. Only Summit Lock 2 and the Summit Division remain before reaching the Chicago River.

Glenwood Stage, 14,000 years ago.

The Des Plaines valley narrows as it passes through the Valparaiso Moraine, another accumulation of till left behind by the Wisconsin Glacier. About 14,000 years ago, meltwater from the retreating glacier formed ancient Lake Chicago to the east, and eventually two outlets, the Des Plaines and Sag Channels, carved their way through. For thousands of years a body of water, that would later become the Great Lakes, drained through here scouring out the valley and uncovering beds of dolomite, a magnesium rich form of limestone. When the I&M Canal was being dug, the "deep cut" plan was hindered by this rock, but it also provided a wealth of building material.

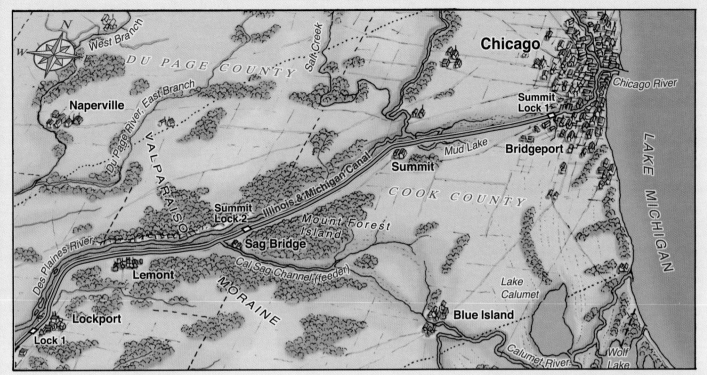

Lockport to Bridgeport.

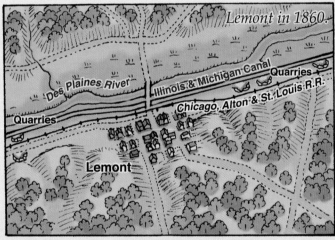

Lemont in 1860.

Reaching the town of Lemont, the *Prairie Star* halts for the night. Lemont was originally founded as Athens, an allusion to the quantities of dolomite found nearby which could be polished and marketed as "Athens Marble." Numerous quarries have been established by local contractors and immigrants who once dug the canal with pick and shovel. They now do the backbreaking work of stone excavation. They are Irish, Welsh, Germans, and Canadians. The lower side of the village, now renamed Lemont, has taken the character of a frontier mining town, with saloons and other establishments to separate quarrymen from their hard-earned pay. The town citizens up on the hill usually avoid this place, especially after dark.

LEMONT STONE QUARRY

At first light, Captain Dawson hires one last mule team and driver which will pull the *Prairie Star* all the way to Bridgeport on the Chicago River. Soon after leaving Lemont, tall wooden derricks beside the canal come into view and then a pit reveals itself, carved into the hillside. The sound of iron being hammered on stone is clearly audible over the water. This is a stone quarry excavating Lemont Limestone, also known as Joliet Limestone, a yellowish-bluish dolomite stone deposited in layers 440 million years ago.

One group pounds iron bars to make indentations, while another man hammer in wedges to split the stone apart.

The limestone beds were uncovered when the I&M Canal was under construction. Canal engineers soon realized that it could be cut into dimensional blocks for the locks, and the stone was readily available right where the canal was being built. Once the I&M was completed, the stone could be transported in barges and it became popular as a building material.

Wagon for moving blocks.

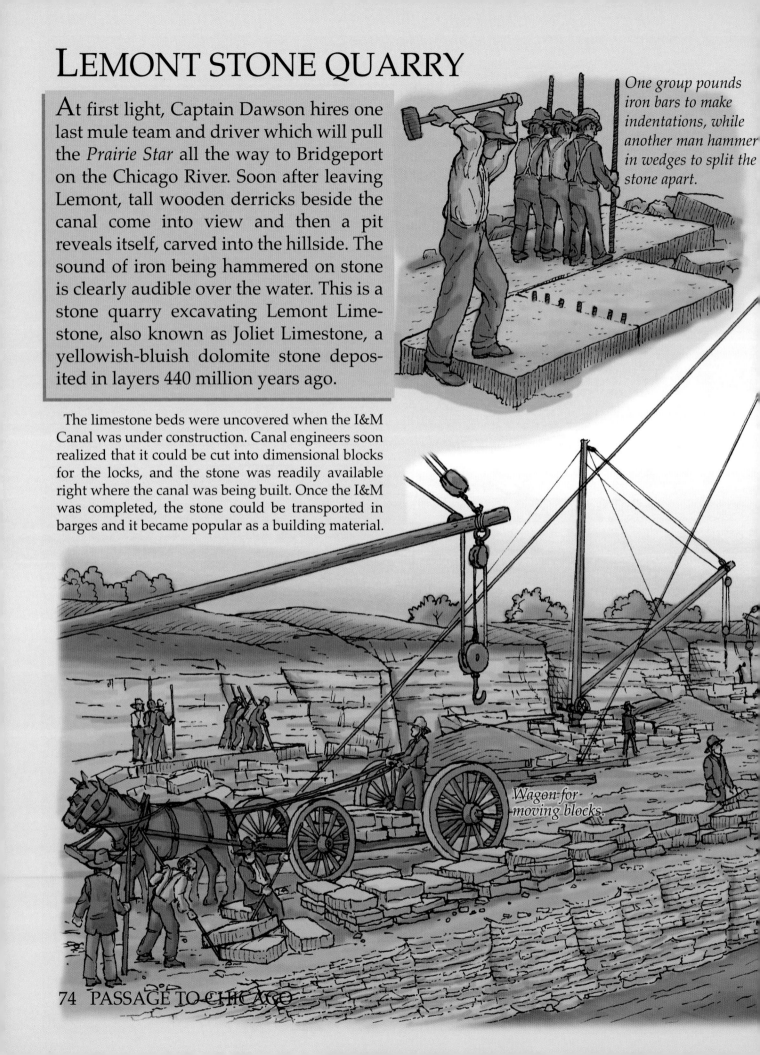

Scores of quarries have been established between Joliet and Sag Bridge by local entrepreneurs like Lorenzo Sanger and George Gaylord, who also owns a dry goods store in Lockport. Immigrant labor drawn to the area to work on the canal is readily available and cheap. The dolomite layers near the surface are thinner and stone taken from here is mainly used for building foundations and for making lime. Further down the stone beds become thicker and are more suitable to be cut into dimensional stone blocks.

Work in a quarry is exhausting and dangerous and the pay is poor even by the standards of the day. The men work in teams; a group lines up with long iron bars that are pounded repeatedly into the stone surface until indentations are made. Then iron wedges are inserted and a quarryman with a heavy sledgehammer drives them in, splitting the stone which is then pried up from its bed. Swinging a sledgehammer all day long and moving the heavy stone blocks is grueling work.

Once removed, the stone is loaded onto specially made wagons and hauled to the bank where it is lifted by hand-powered derricks, and carefully swung onto the decks of canal barges. The blocks are incredibly heavy; it is easy for an accident to occur and a man to be crushed or badly injured. Work in the quarries is seasonal and as soon as the snow begins to fall the quarrymen are out of a job for months with no way to support their families.

The typical canal boat can carry a limited amount of stone on deck, but heavy loads demand a better kind of boat with a deeper reinforced deck that lowers the center of gravity to carry more stone.

Gin pole derrick

Blocks being loaded on a canal barge.

Lime kilns

SAG BRIDGE TO MUD LAKE

St James at Sag Bridge

Rising up ahead is the mass of Mount Forest Island, a large wooded elevation, and part of Valparaiso Moraine. This place was once very much an island when the Des Plaines River and Cal Sag Channel were enormous drainage channels for glacial Lake Chicago. This morning the scene is quiet and beautiful with the fall colors nearing their peak. At the junction of the I&M and the Cal Sag feeder is the little Irish community of Sag Bridge. On the hillside above the town is their church, Saint James at Sag Bridge.

Saint James is a Catholic Church founded in 1833 by Irish immigrants who worked on the I&M Canal and then settled in this place. Originally it was only a log cabin, but the people have raised the money to build a new church made of Lemont Limestone, many of them helping haul the blocks to the site. Saint James is a mission church with a priest coming from Chicago on horseback every three months.

Beyond Sag Bridge is Summit Lock 2, also known as Jack's Lock. Here the *Prairie Star* is raised to the Summit Level of the canal that will take her all the way to Bridgeport. Beyond Mount Forest Island, the canal enters the Chicago Lake Plain and the Village of Summit which lies on the watershed between the

Mississippi River valley and the Great Lakes basin. This is the highest point on the canal, and water from the pumping station at Bridgeport, over 10 miles away, is sometimes insufficient to maintain proper depth. The mule teams often have to work harder here getting the boats across.

Past Summit, the canal crosses Mud Lake, a marshy remnant of the glacial runoff channel. In wet years, a channel sometimes re-establishes the connection. For centuries Native Americans traveled through here, and during the fur trade era, Mud Lake was part of the Chicago portage. Marquette and Joliet were the first to propose it as a site for a canal, and later, the canoe brigades of the American Fur Trade Company used the portage on the way to and from Michilimackinac. Gurdon S. Hubbard traveled the portage with one of the brigades in 1818 at the age of 16 and spent many years in Illinois as a fur trader and land speculator. Later he opened the first meat packing plant in Chicago. Hubbard was an advocate of the canal and as a state legislator helped ensure it ended at the Chicago River, not the Calumet, pointing out that a great city would rise at its terminus and Illinois should not share it with Indiana.

In the early days of the canal, when packet boats were crossing Mud Lake in the summer, their crews would close all the windows and shutters to keep out miasmas and fevers. The passengers would have

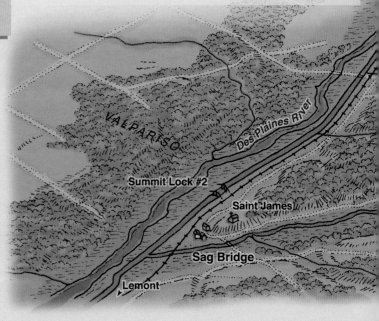

to swelter in the main cabin, but given the fear of diseases like typhoid and cholera they endured it.

In 1860 Mud Lake is still largely unchanged and during the summer months the heat and mosquitoes often make it miserable for the canalers. Today at least the cool fall weather has put an end to the insects. The *Prairie Star* is now close enough to Chicago to see the chimney smoke rising above the marsh grass. The traffic on the canal here is heavy with grain and coal barges headed into the city and lumber boats coming out. Ann takes the tiller while her husband and son Charlie help the bowsman.

Crossing Mud Lake on the way to Bridgeport.

LAKE MICHIGAN

Chicago River Mouth

Chicago

Summit Lock #1

Bridgeport

Mud Lake

Illinois & Michigan Canal (Summit Level)

Archer Avenue

Summit

Mount Forest Island

Sag Channel (feeder)

BRIDGEPORT

At last the *Prairie Star* arrives at Bridgeport and the eastern terminus of the I&M. At Summit Lock 1 she will be lowered down to the Chicago River, where Captain Dawson can hire a tow to Wolf Point and the elevator to which he has been contracted to deliver his corn. First he must wait for a boat ahead and a lumber barge entering the canal from the river.

Charlie Dawson and Eric Lindgren sit on the gunwale at bow and marvel at the city that lies beyond the lock, evident from the smoke in the air and the throngs of people and wagons. Ships' masts rising over the tops of buildings show that it is a great port as well. Most of the population here are Irish who came to work on the canal and settled in Bridgeport.

Near the lock is the Bridgeport Pumping Station, an engineering marvel. It uses some of the most powerful water pumps west of the Appalachians, fed by massive steam boilers. The station is in continuous operation pumping water from the Chicago River to fill the Summit level of the Canal. The city is so proud of this facility that just last month, Mayor John Wentworth brought the 19-year old Prince of Wales and future King Edward VII of England, to tour this mechanical wonder during his visit to Chicago.

There are many businesses in Bridgeport that thrive on the canal traffic: saloons, hotels, grocery stores, blacksmiths, harness makers, mule barns, and livery stables. Along the north bank of the South Branch of the Chicago River is an enormous lumber district, dwarfing any of the yards on the canal. Slips allow schooners to unload their cargoes of Michigan and Wisconsin pine to add to the stacks of lumber already there. Canal barges use the same slips to load lumber to take down the canal. Dredges work on new slips, but there is still a shortage of dock space.

Beside the lock is one last toll house. The toll collector for Chicago is John Kinzie, who as a child growing up at his father's trading post can remember when Chicago was little more than Fort Dearborn, a collection of log cabins and a few taverns.

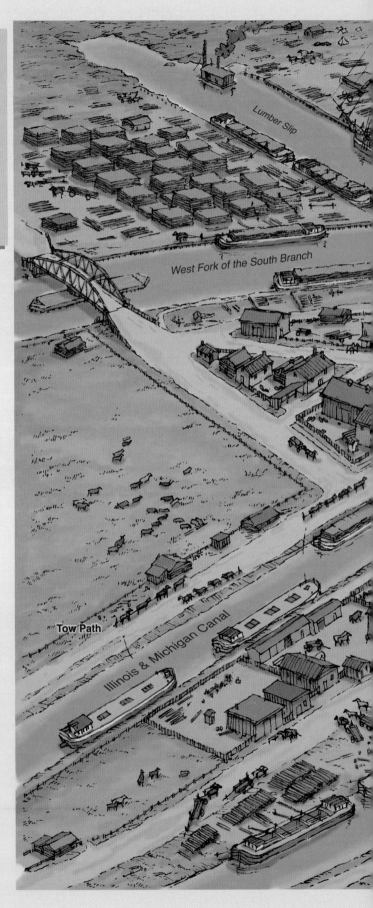

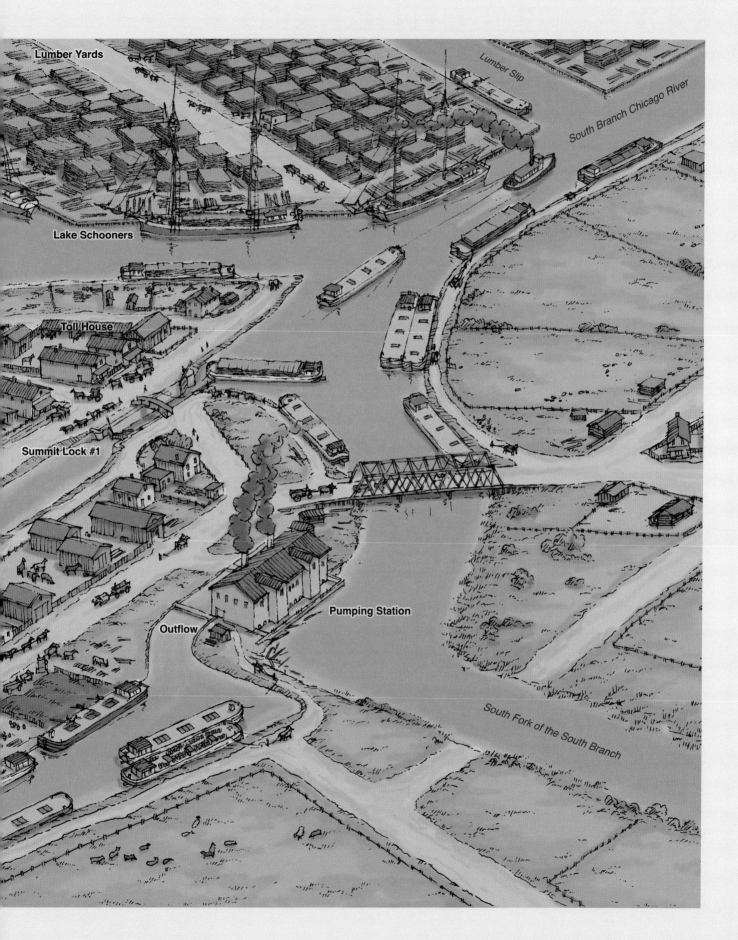

Lumber Yards

Lumber Slip

South Branch Chicago River

Lake Schooners

Toll House

Summit Lock #1

Pumping Station

Outflow

South Fork of the South Branch

DOWN THE SOUTH BRANCH

Once out of the lock the *Prairie Star* ties up with other barges waiting for a tow down the South Branch of the Chicago River. The boat is headed to Wolf Point where the north and south branches of the river meet, and an elevating warehouse where the corn is to be delivered. The mule team is led away to a mule barn in Bridgeport. There is no room for towpaths along the river front; any vessels lacking steam power must be moved by a fleet of small propeller-driven tugs that dart about like water bugs.

Eventually Captain Dawson is able to hire a tug and Eric Lindgren casts a tow rope over to it. Smoke pours out of the powerful little vessel as its propeller churns the water and the rope goes taut; the *Prairie Star* begins to move slowly down the crowded river.

The growth of Chicago in just 25 years has been astounding. In 1860, the population is over 100,000 and the city's economic power can clearly be seen from the river. Enormous grain elevators, lumberyards, and other enterprises of brick and balloon-frame construction, crowd in around docks which are lined with vessels of every description.

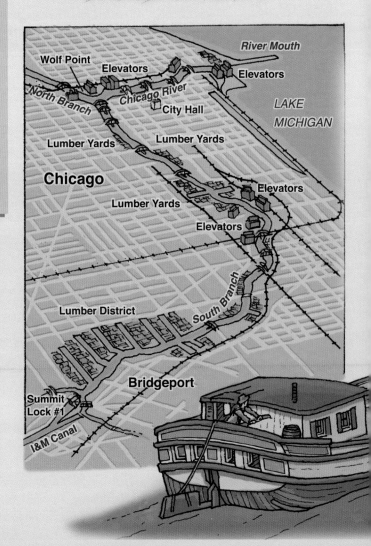

From the window of the *Prairie Star's* cabin, Charlie and Maggie gaze at the graceful lake schooners with streamlined bows and soaring masts. There are more prosaic scow schooner types as well, and brigs from an earlier era on the lakes. There are large steamboats, side-wheelers and propellor vessels that carry passengers and immigrants across the Great Lakes from as far away as Buffalo. Steam-powered dredges in the river deepen the channel and dig new slips.

Beyond the river the presence of the railroad makes itself known with steam trains moving about blowing their whistles. Rail lines pass beside all of the elevators and many of the lumberyards.

A tug pulls the Prairie Star past a line of schooners and side-wheel steamboats, drawn up beside massive grain elevators. Most Great Lakes crews are Scandinavian immigrants, usually experienced sailors who naturally gravitate to this job. There are also many Irish and German immigrants ready to work on the lake boats.

At Lake Street, there is a final delay waiting for several swing bridges to open. These are large timber truss bridges that swing open in a circle for river traffic to pass through. The needs of the port exist in an uneasy balance with the needs of the city. Great traffic jams of wagons and pedestrian foot traffic wait in front of bridges held open for vessels to pass. The reverse is true when the lake boats and canal barges must wait for the wagon traffic. As the port of Chicago continues to grow, this problem only gets worse.

WOLF POINT, JOURNEY'S END

built its first true elevator in 1852 and now has 12 of them, moving close to 50 million bushels a year. Chicago is the largest grain port in the world.

At the base of the elevator the hatches are opened to be examined by an inspector while Captain Dawson looks on. Ann and Maggie watch from behind the cabin on the steering deck, although Maggie seems more interested in the seagulls crying and circling overhead who are looking for an opportunity to snatch some kernels of corn.

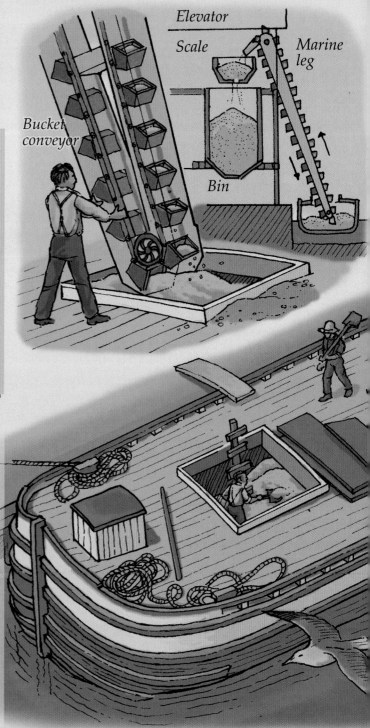

Elevator
Scale
Marine leg
Bucket conveyor
Bin

The last swing bridge is passed and the *Prairie Star* finally arrives under tow at Wolf Point. A large turning basin makes room for the enormous volume of traffic that passes through here, where the north and south branches of the Chicago River meet. The tug takes the *Prairie Star* across the basin to a large elevator on the north bank and casts off, giving her enough headway for the steersman to maneuver to the dock below the towering structure.

The first modern grain elevator was built in 1842 by Joseph Dart in Buffalo; however, the grain elevator system was perfected in Chicago. In the 1850s the Chicago Board of Trade devised the grading method, allowing commingling of the same grades and types of grain. This allowed grain to be moved in great quantities by mechanical means inside the elevators. Meanwhile, the telegraph allowed buyers and sellers to make transactions without the buyer seeing the grain he was purchasing. They simply agreed on a price for an amount of grain of a certain grade to be delivered on a certain date. The delivery of corn by the *Prairie Star* from an elevator in Ottawa to one in Chicago is completing one such contract. Chicago

After the inspector's approval, workers position a large marine "leg" over a hatch and lower it into the corn. The leg has a steam-powered bucket conveyor belt that digs into the corn and raises it into the elevator to be dumped into a receiving hopper and weighed. Nothing moves in an elevator without being weighed; hopefully, the final tally will agree with the amount loaded in Ottawa. The corn is then sorted into bins and stored. At some point, it will be off-loaded into a lake vessel and sailed across the Great Lakes to another elevator at Buffalo, then moved by rail or the Erie Canal to New York City.

At last, the journey of the *Prairie Star* is complete. Captain Dawson receives his shipping fee and he pays his first mate; Charlie is still too young to receive wages. For many bargemen, this is an opportunity to disappear into the saloons and other attractions found in Chicago, spending all their money before hiring on again with another boat. However, Eric Lindgren will remain with the boat.

Captain Dawson hires a tug to take the *Prairie Star* back to Bridgeport and the lumber district, to load pine boards for a return trip down the canal. The boat will make several more journeys like this before season's end.

A marine "leg" is positioned over one of the holds.

Gulls circle overhead, hoping to snatch a bit of corn as the Prairie Star is unloaded. Workers in the hold shovel corn into piles for bucket conveyor.

POSTSCRIPT

It is late December 1860 and the *Prairie Star* is in the Steamboat Basin opposite the town of Peru. It sits in company with a number of other canal boats as a snow storm begins to pick up strength. The Illinois & Michigan Canal is closed now, its water drained away for the winter. All is quiet as the snow begins to cover the idle boat decks, but in the world outside, great events are now stirring.

Since the *Prairie Star's* journey to Chicago in October, Abraham Lincoln has been elected to the presidency, although he won't depart Illinois for several months yet. However, for many southern states his election is seen as a direct threat to their way of life, and South Carolina has already voted to secede from the Union. There is now talk of civil war.

Great changes will occur on the Illinois & Michigan Canal during the years of conflict that are to follow. The canal will carry more cargo than ever before as it helps supply the Union armies. But people in the towns and farms along its banks will also learn the tragedy of war, with the growing casualty lists including the names of many canalers.

The Illinois & Michigan Canal will serve for another half-century before dwindling traffic and neglect finally close it down. By then, other waterways will be in operation. The Illinois Waterway, a system of locks and dams, will make the Illinois River navigable all the way to Joliet where it will join the Sanitary & Ship Canal and the Cal Sag Channel, connecting with Lake Michigan. The new waterways will be traveled by vessels and tows of sizes barely imagined by the crew of the *Prairie Star*. But the canal tradition begun in Illinois by the I&M Canal and experienced by boats like the *Prairie Star* will continue on well into the future.